Parker, America's Finest Shotgun

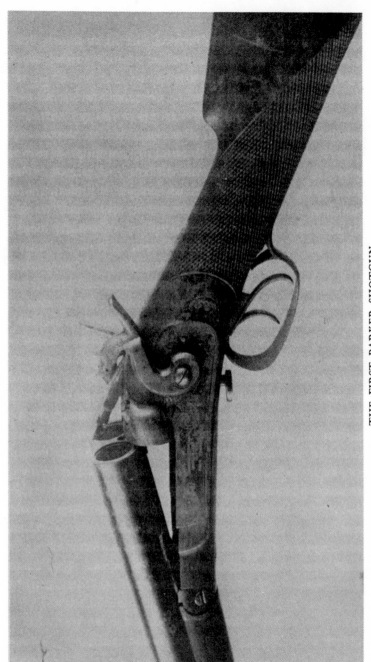

THE FIRST PARKER SHOTGUN.

Parker

America's Finest Shotgun

By Peter H. Johnson

BONANZA BOOKS · NEW YORK

*Dedicated to the
Men and Women, Living
and Dead, Who, as
the Skilled and
Dedicated Employees
of Parker, Made the
Parker America's
Finest Shotgun*

*"Much care is bestowed to make it
what the Sportsmen need—a good gun."*

—CHARLES PARKER

Contents

Preface

This book is, in a sense, the product of a lifetime of interest in guns and shooting. Although it has been a comparatively short lifetime, it has, nonetheless, been quite sufficient to provide a very wide variety of experience in the study of all types of firearms, among the most interesting of which is certainly the shotgun. I have, in recent years especially, made as wide a study of guns and related subjects as my work and the necessary opportunities afforded. In this respect I have been very fortunate in that I have, for the greater part of my life, been a resident of the nation's capital, where opportunities for the study of guns and weapons of many kinds abound.

It was not in Washington, however, that my interest in the particular gun which forms the subject of this book originated, but rather in my home town when I was very young indeed. This life-long interest in the Parker Gun, the origin of which I shall say more about in the Introduction, was thus a part of the very first contact I experienced with guns and shooting.

It has only been during the past several years, however, that my interest and that of the public have grown to an extent that seemed to make a specialized study of this particular make of shotgun desirable and possible.

For all the assistance, advice, suggestions, information and encouragement I received in my study and preparation of material on the Parker Gun and the writing of this book, I owe a debt of gratitude to several persons, in particular to Mr. Charles Stuart Parker, great-grandson of the founder of the industrial firm which produced the Parker Gun. Mr. Parker, who was the last president of Parker Brothers, very generously provided me with the technical details concerning the production of Parker Guns, in addition to many interesting details concerning the company, its business operations, and the Parker family. For the time and effort which this entailed, I am particularly grateful.

I wish, in addition, to express my thanks to the following officials of Remington Arms Company who gave me every possible help and assistance in securing old Parker data and information on the gun after it was purchased by Remington: to Mr. S. M. Alvis, Manager, Ilion Research Division, for receiving my requests for help and passing them on to the right persons; to Mr. A. D. Kerr, of the Ilion Planning Section, whose knowledge of Parker Guns, coming from personal participation in the acquirement of Parker by Remington, and kind efforts to secure what information on the Parker is still available, were of the greatest assistance to me in preparing the chapters on the final history of the gun; to Mr. Frank Cashman of the Arms Service Unit and Mr. Gail Evans, Director of Sales, for providing interesting details about the identification marks used on Parkers and facts about Parker catalogs; to Mr. Robert P. Runge of the Arms Service Unit for the loan of old magazine material. To Abercrombie and Fitch of New York. To Von Lengerke and Antoine of Chicago. To Mr. Glover

A. Snow of Meriden, Conn. To Col. Eric F. Storm (Ret.) of Fairhaven, Vermont. To Mrs. Elizabeth L. Hanson of Old Saybrook, Conn. To Mr. H. L. Carpenter of Herkimer, N.Y. And finally to Mrs. Betty deAtley for her patience in the typing of the manuscript.

For all the efforts made by the above-named persons, without which this book would not have been possible, I am very grateful.

Washington, D.C.

Introduction

The history of firearms presents a curious yet strangely familiar pattern of changes in taste and preference. A fundamental design of gun mechanism, one calculated to give the utmost in service and satisfaction to the user, yet capable of the most refined and artistic decoration and finish, will, in the course of time, become obsolete and be superseded by something fundamentally less perfect in conception and much less adapted to artistic workmanship; and then, after a period of time, the former design gradually becomes an object of, first, purely historical interest, next of enthusiastic contrast and comparison on the part of collectors and students, and, finally, if sufficient public interest is aroused, is manufactured anew to supply a demand that is partly enthusiasm, partly practical need, and, to an extent, pure sentimental attachment.

This is true not only of guns, but of any mechanical object that has caught the eye and aroused the enthusiasm of man, and ended by capturing his imagination. It is true of man's favorite mechanical contrivance, the automobile. One frequently hears of the Stanley Steamer as the best car ever made in the U.S. This may or may not be true; but what is without doubt true is that, should a few of them be remade to the original design, there would be a fairly large number of people quite willing to pay a very fancy price for the privilege of owning one. And the Duesenberg! What is by almost unanimous consent America's finest car is a prized collector's pride and enthusiastically hailed at the same time as the greatest auto design ever produced in America. After World War II, an attempt was actually made to reissue this classic auto, but production costs were much too high to make it even remotely possible. An original Duesenberg today brings a very fancy price indeed and is the pride and joy of its owner. It would not be at all surprising if, at some time in the near future, one of the old favorite classic designs of automobile should be remade and become a financial success for the entrepreneur.

This cycle of oblivion and resurrection is certainly to be witnessed in the public's attitude toward the iron horse of mechanical perfection, the steam locomotive. At present, when the railroads are all converting to Diesel and Electric engines, before the steam engine has even been finally relegated to the locomotive graveyard, nostalgic complaints of sorrow and regret may be heard concerning the passing away of what has been, for so long, part of the American scene. One inevitably hears, along with these sighs of regret, the assertion of the mechanical superiority and durability of the steam engine in comparison with any other type. And despite the fact that in this realm economic influence on such a large scale makes resurrection an impossibility, the model railroad enthusiasts have already made it quite clear that the great age of steam railroading will be with us for a long time to come, that it will, in fact, be permanently preserved in the superbly fine model engines that are appearing on the market in ever larger number and variety.

But in almost no realm of public interest in the mechanical arts is this cycle of death and glorious resurrection so frequently and astonishingly apparent as that of firearms design and production. The war changed this aspect of weapon making, as it did all other forms of manufacturing, causing the almost complete cessation of civilian weapon production while at the same time creating the largest demand for, and inevitably the largest interest in, guns of all types in human history. With the coming of peace, many of the older models of shotguns, rifles and pistols were dropped from the production schedule, apparently never to be returned.

But then a strange thing happened. Within three years of the war's end, many of the gun and sporting goods magazines were featuring articles dealing with such old favorite models as the Frontier Colt, the Colt pocket automatics, the German Luger and Mauser, and the more popular sporting guns that had been withdrawn from the catalogs. In the case of the first mentioned of these weapons, the Colt Frontier Revolver, the advent of television and the resulting vogue for western lore and legend that soon swept the country were quite sufficient to create a demand for the restoring of this old-time favorite to the Colt line. Colt complied in 1955 and today the Frontier or Peacemaker is one of the best selling of all the Colt models. Colt's smallest pistol, the .25 automatic, has made a similar if not so spectacular comeback. And I think there is very little doubt indeed that, were it mechanically and legally possible for Germany to remake the Luger, that outstanding hand gun would have a world-wide sale in larger quantities than ever.

This interesting reversion, in many ways quite as practical as it is nostalgic, has not been perhaps so obvious in regard to the most common and widely used of all firearms, the shotgun. But it is nonetheless present and particularly so at the present time when there are more people of all ages enjoying man's primal sport, hunting, than ever before. All circumstances considered, it is therefore quite inevitable that there should be a revival of interest in that basic and still supreme achievement in gun design, the double barrel shotgun.

Not that there has ever been a definite lapse of interest in what has very properly been called the nearest thing to the perfect gun ever designed. Indeed, one can hardly conceive of the time ever coming when the old reliable double will be outdated. As Shakespeare said of Cleopatra, "Time cannot stale nor custom wither [its] infinite variety." And it is that same variety rather than any particular model or aspect of design that forms the focus of the current swing of interest and enthusiasm back to the double. For as no other type of firearm has been more widely used than the double, certainly no other has appeared, in every corner of the globe, in a wider variety of quality and style, a variety ranging from the absolute peak of the gunmaker's art and craft to the lowest specimen of makeshift junk that any so-called maker would dare to put on the market. And yet, it is a strange but significant fact that even in the cases of the most palpably crude and poor quality guns, the double mechanism is seldom if ever a complete failure. Many of the cheapest and commonest of the mass production doubles, sold by the mail order houses in enormous quantities all over the U.S. and Canada, are still in use and can be found in cabins, barns, outhouses and attics all over the nation, and are still bringing down the bacon.

The variety of double guns made in the United States, however, has, in the past twenty years, been reduced by the war, consequent economic changes and a shift in preference to the repeater, to an almost infinitesimal number. At the time of the writing of this book, there are but two qualities of the double barrel shotgun still made in America, but the great difference in quality to which this design is susceptible of adaptation is astonishingly revealed in these two lines. We have made here at present the Stevens-Fox on the one hand and the famous Winchester Model 21 on the other. The former is the product of one of the oldest of our gun makers and one whose career has been marked by quantity production of low priced but reliable arms, while the latter is the most expensive and meticulously made of all the guns put out by what is perhaps the most widely known name in the field of weapon making in the world. The Winchester Model 21 is certainly an expensive shotgun and always has been, but now it is apparently destined to become not merely a very high grade example in its class, but a strictly luxury gun. I have recently been informed by one of Winchester's top production men that the various grades of the Model 21 will soon be eliminated and that it will then be produced only on special order and at a cost of around twelve hundred dollars. This, of course, is just another example of the fact that a truly first class model of a double gun requires the utmost in craftsmanship and mechanical skill to produce—and in our present day of highly paid labor, Winchester has apparently found that it is not economically feasible to make such a product except for the most limited demand and then only as one which is made on an all or nothing at all basis.

But this was not always the situation in the United States in regard to the double barrel shotgun. There was a time, a rather extensive period of time, when the entire matter stood on practically the opposite basis. In the latter part of the Nineteenth Century, there arose, almost simultaneously, a half dozen firms whose specialty was the making of double barrel shotguns, in grades ranging from the most ordinary to the best that it was possible to produce. It is not surprising that among the first makers of fine double guns the name Colt stands out. This world-renowned firm, producers of the first successful revolver, marketed for a few years a splendid double barrel shotgun whose lines of grace and elegance and whose mechanical superiority well represented the standard that has, from the beginning, been associated with the name Colt. But Colt's destiny was in the making of revolvers and pistols as Winchester's was in rifles and shotguns and both firms very wisely struck out early in the particular line of gun making for which the future seemed to promise them success. Certainly neither firm went wrong in making this decision and their names have risen to be household words the world over in their respective lines of weapon manufacture.

But for those firms whose specialty was the double gun, the golden age lay just ahead. By 1895, the thirty years since the end of the Civil War had brought success to what came, in the course of time, to be the big six of the makers of double barrel shotguns. Whenever the subject of hunting or shooting arose, one almost inevitably heard one or more of the following names mentioned: Parker, Fox, Ithaca, L. C. Smith, Lefever, Baker any one of these stood for a good shotgun—one that was dependable and of a recognizably superior quality, and these names held the field. With the exception of the Baker, which ceased manufacture in the 1920's, all the remaining five companies, in the form of either independent firms or subsidiaries, maintained their position as the top makers of fine doubles until the beginning of World War II and with that conflict, this product, like so many good things of the past with its more leisurely way of life, passed into history. It is true that Ithaca and L.C. Smith made a very few doubles after the war, Ithaca even bringing out some of its famous 10 gauge magnums; but the post-war economy was not equipped to sustain such a product and Ithaca, by 1950, had converted entirely to repeaters while Smith became an affiliate of Marlin and then went out of business altogether. The name Fox does survive in one moderately priced double made by Stevens—Savage, the latter firm having acquired the Fox Company when it went out of business in the late twenties and after the war merged with Stevens. Of Lefever practically nothing is now heard, but memories of Uncle Dan's shotgun will last for a long time.

Of all the various names of gunmakers mentioned so far, however, there is one which, in the world of shotguns, has from the beginning held first place. Mention of its name still evokes a ready and enthusiastic response of recognition as America's finest shotgun. I first became acquainted with the name during my first acquaintance with guns and shooting in general. I was born on a Mississippi plantation, near the famous old Civil War town of Vicksburg. Thus, from my earliest days, I can remember the sight of guns and shells around me in the house, the old trademarks of the rising sun on Remington shell boxes, and the big X on Western, the sound of gun shots in the woods echoing across the countryside, and the smell of powder on a crisp fall morning on those rare occasions when my grandfather or uncles had reason to fire their guns in the backyard, usually at my request. Among these and many other memories which rise so often with the nostalgic grandeur of the years, one stands out with vivid clarity, and it is this one which may rightfully be called the germ of this book.

One evening, on a cold and dark fall night, as my grandparents were preparing for bed and my mother was trying to persuade me to do the same, a knock at the door brought us all into the living room. Our nocturnal visitor was Dr. Bryant Cook, a local physician and planter, whose favorite sport was hunting and shooting and who had the well-deserved reputation of being the most expert hunter in the area. He had had a successful day in the field, and, on his way home, had stopped by to see my grandfather and give him some of the partridges which had fallen to his gun.

So, as the Doctor and my grandfather went into the kitchen to examine the birds and put them into the icebox, I took the opportunity to examine the Doctor's gun, which he had placed in a corner of the living room. There was something about it which appealed to me instantly. Not that there was anything new about a double barrel shotgun. Even at the age of six, I was well aware that it was the most commonly-found type of gun in existence and therefore the most popular. I had seen many of them, and, before seeing this one, they had all looked very much alike to me. But this one was different. My first thought as I carefully scrutinized the gun, while keeping a respectful distance, was "Boy, that's really a neat double," which is only a youngster's way of saying, "That double has something to mark it out as special, different from others of the same kind." At about this time, as my grandfather and his guest emerged from the kitchen, I greeted them with the observation "Say, Dr. Cook, that's really a nice looking gun you've got." He answered "It's sure that all right and it's not only nice looking it's nice shooting; but anyway, Peter, that's not just a shotgun, that's a *Parker*."

This emphatic endorsement of the Parker as something distinct and apart, in a class all by itself, given by the neighborhood's most respected hunter and sportsman, was my introduction to what I was as the time thus made fully aware was the very best it was possible to obtain in a shotgun. From then on, I heard the name Parker often and always with the same connotation: there is nothing finer than a Parker. A present-day Parker owner, who, like so many others, treasures his Parkers as family heirlooms, is Mr. Forrest E. Kellow of Oregon. His favorite metaphor for them, "the old jewels", is most fitting and appropriate.

I have since learned that the years had given their approval to the Doctor's opinion of his gun, and that thousands of sportsmen in the U.S., Canada, and foreign countries have enthusiastically shared it.

But time brings many changes, and perhaps it has brought more to the field of gun design than any field of mechanical invention. So it was that with the inventions of John Browning, America's greatest gun wizard, and the world's greatest inventor of repeating firearms, the pump action and automatic shotgun found a ready and enthusiastic market in North America. Two reasons account for this popularity of the repeating shotgun in this part of the world: the natural preference of residents of the Western Hemisphere area for inventions and designs of the most advanced type, particularly in the area of gun design (although this might appear to be denied by such gross oversights as the rejection of the Luger by U.S. factories and the U.S. Government), and the actual topographical and biological factors governing hunting in North America especially—large, sometimes limitless areas of hunting country of varying terrain, and what was, at one time at least, an almost limitless supply of game.

But here as in all other areas the pendulum must swing when a balance is not maintained, so by the middle 1930's, when the repeater was by far the most popular type of shotgun and more people than ever before were hunting, game and conservation authorities of both the federal and state governments realized the need for cutting down on the firepower of shotguns as a measure necessary to conservation. This brought the regulation requiring a plug for the magazines of all repeating shotguns which limited their capacity to a total of three shots, plus severer bag limits for all types of game hunting. This reduction of shell capacity to three did not, however, reduce the popularity of repeating shotguns. A generation of hunters had become used to them and that one extra shell was of sufficient value in the opinion of the vast majority to make a repeater, even with a plugged magazine, still the most desirable and practical type of sporting gun. This preference for the repeater, plus the coming of the war, brought an end to the production of double guns in the United States, and the end of the war saw the revival of but two or three out of the entire pre-war line.

But with the passage of time, the pendulum has swung in the opposite direction, and we are now witnessing a great revival of interest in the classic American doubles and in the Parker in particular. Once again the name Parker has come to mean in the minds of this generation of gun lovers what the name Duesenberg once meant in the minds of another generation of automobile lovers, and many a sportsman and collector is anxious to own the American shotgun of which it may be said as Macaulay said of Boswell's *Life of Johnson* among biographies: "Eclipse is first, and the rest nowhere."

CHAPTER 1

Background and Origin of the Parker Company

THE COMPANY which perfected and produced America's finest shotgun had its origin, as did so many other American gun makers, in the early years of the nation's independence in the region and in the particular state which still produces the great majority of the nation's sporting weapons. The Parker Gun originated, was perfected, and produced for the full span of its independent existence in Connecticut, the state which is still known as America's Arsenal. The career of the man who became the father of this premier product of American gun making and the circumstances surrounding the creation of the gun itself are typical, even symbolic, of the spirit and daring of early American industry and in the finest traditions of our nation's system of free enterprise.

Charles Parker, whose surname has come to symbolize the best that it is possible to produce in a shotgun, was a native New Englander, descended from the earliest English settlers in that region. He was born January 2, 1809, in Cheshire, Connecticut, and began what was to be an extraordinarily long and successful career as an industrialist in the then traditional manner of an apprentice. This apprenticeship was in the casting of but-

13

tons in a small factory in Southington, Connecticut, and though begun at an early age was apparently quite sufficient to determine the young man in the choice of his life's career. While still what is today called a teen-ager, he arrived in the town where he was to become

CHARLES PARKER.

a successful industrialist in typical Yankee fashion and to later establish his famous gun factory.

Coming to Meriden in 1828, he hired himself out with a Patrick Lewis to make coffee mills. This product must have held his interest in a special way or, what may be more likely, he realized with the unerring sense of values that characterized his career, that here was a product in which he could achieve success through quality. In any case, within four years of his employment with Lewis, he was ready to start his own business; and that he did, in the best Horatio Alger fashion, with a capital outlay of $70.00, establishing his original firm in 1832. And how well that firm represents the pioneering spirit of early American industry. Charles Parker's first power plant was a blind horse hitched to a pole sweep but this primitive yet apparently quite successful means of power production, after twelve years of productive capacity, was succeeded in 1844, by the first steam engine in the vicinity.

By this time, the population of New England, especially the southern section, was growing apace and Charles Parker's awareness of its needs led him to begin his expansion into what was eventually to become an almost incredible number of products. The Parker Company Catalog of 1862 lists the amazing total of several hundred items, among which are such staple hardware varieties as corn and coffee mills, German silver tableware, silvered tobacco tins, cigar and spectacle cases, vises, hinges, grindstone rollers, door knockers, locks, pump elevators, waffle irons and many other things which no doubt found a ready market among the people of that period. The rather wide extent of this market is clearly revealed by the story of a sailor on the good ship *James Littlefield* who tells of seeing Parker coffee mills displayed in Melbourne, Australia, as early as 1859.

The catalog mentioned above included the products of other local factories in which Parker very likely already had some financial interest or for which he was no doubt acting as distributor, several of which later became subsidiaries of his own firm. In years following the company entered even more enterprises, including the manufacture of larger and more precision-built products such as steam engines, printing presses, and machine tools.

This extensive scale of manufacturing naturally led to several mergers and business combinations, one of which was destined to become the source of the Parker

The factory at Meriden, Connecticut, before the firm name read Parker, Snow, Brooks & Company. The reproduction is from a wood cut presumably made sometime prior to the year 1860

shotgun. This was the partnership with the Snow machine works. The story of this rather interesting business firm is as follows:

In 1839, seven years after Charles Parker had begun his first business venture, two brothers, Oliver and Heman Snow, started a general machine jobbing business. In two or three years Heman decided to withdraw from the firm and sold his share to Lucas L. Hotchkiss, after which the firm was called Snow and Hotchkiss. In 1844 Charles Parker came in as a partner and the firm became Snow, Hotchkiss and Company. One year later Hotchkiss withdrew and the name changed to Oliver Snow and Company, after which for the next nine years the firm made machinery of all kinds.

A joint stock company was then formed under the name of Meriden Machine Company, which employed 120 men in the smithy, machine shop and foundry. One of the stockholders and superintendents in this firm was Gamaliel F. Snow. In 1854 more capital was put into the firm and it expanded under still another name, Snow, Brooks and Company. It was this last-named firm, in which Charles Parker still retained some interest as a partner and stockholder, which received a contract during the Civil War for rifles for the Union Army. Few were actually turned out as the war ended before production could get well under way; but what was turned out, in addition to being the ancestor proper of the Parker Gun, retains a very definite interest as a firearm in its own right; and more will be said about it in the next chapter.

It was Gamaliel F. Snow, apparently an important official of the firm both mechanically and financially at this period, who laid out the buildings which the firm occupied at the time these Civil War rifles were made, and which came to be the ones occupied later by Parker when the company was organized to make sporting weapons, and which it continued to occupy for the remainder of its existence. The majority of these factory buildings in which the Parker gun was made are still standing, having been acquired by the International Silver Company for addition to that firm's plant when

One of The Charles Parker Company's first-quality products—a double-grinder, box-type coffee mill.

Parker as an independent firm went out of business in 1934.

At the time of the Civil War the name of the firm was Parker, Snow, Brooks and Company; but by the war's end it had again changed and this time reverted back to the Meriden Manufacturing Company. But regardless of the name, the firm had for its president in 1865 Charles Parker, who at this time had some half-dozen full-scale manufacturing plants scattered around Meriden, making everything from the famous Parker coffee mills to tin spoons and piano stools and all the other articles mentioned earlier which are to be found in the 1862 Parker Catalog.

The firm continued in this setup for about four years, after which, in 1869, the entire business was sold to, or at least came under the control of, Charles Parker at which time the decision was made to give up many of their other lines and devote themselves to a large extent to the production of sporting guns. The exact reasons causing this decision and the circumstances surrounding the production of the first Parkers are of course matters quite important enough in the history of the Parker gun to deserve a separate chapter. It is certainly not without interest, however, that this chapter on the background of the formation of the Parker gun works may be closed by mentioning the fact that at the time the factory converted to the full-scale manufacture of sporting guns the name Snow had disappeared entirely from the firm's control. Mr. Glover A. Snow, grandson of Gamaliel F. Snow, remarks that it is only to be assumed that the Snows were either very poor business men or that they got squeezed in Yankee horse trading. I think that it can, in any case, be very safely assumed that Mr. Charles Parker had, at the age of sixty, lost none of the business acumen and industrial foresight which had guided him unerringly since the days of the blind horse, and which had now brought him to the threshold of what was to quickly become the manufacture of the finest and most honored shotgun the country had ever seen or very likely ever would see.

CHAPTER 2

Parker During the Civil War

BEFORE TAKING UP the beginning of the Parker shotgun proper, I think it well worthwhile to pause a moment to consider the part played by Parker in the production of guns shortly before and during the Civil War. No record has survived of any weapons of any kind whatever being made by the Parker Company or any of its subsidiaries prior to this time and all indications are that Charles Parker had previously never even attempted to add this kind of hardware to his line. I think it safe to say, however, that the wise old Yankee industrialist had seen quite a bit of the making and merchandising of guns and ammunition components, and no doubt had a very shrewd outlook on the matter sometime before the beginning of the war.

It would, in fact, have been next to impossible for anyone even remotely connected with any kind of manufacturing in the New England area around the middle of the Nineteenth Century to be unaware of the trends and practices in the firearms industry. America was then, as now, a nation of riflemen and gun lovers as it had been since colonial days. The boys at Lexington and Concord had indeed fired the shot heard around the world, another generation had continued firing at New Orleans and the Alamo and still another was just about to fire the largest number of shots up to that time in our

21

nation's history; and out of the flaming fusillade of the Civil War's battlefields was to be welded the strength and unified glory of the United States whose restless urge to move West until all land between the two oceans lay under Old Glory brought the immortal epic of the American frontier, an epic in which guns of every type played an indispensable and glorious role.

An industrialist with the ability and foresight of Charles Parker could not have been oblivious to the demand for firearms for normal peacetime usage and certainly not to the steadily widening western frontier market which, even before the Civil War, had begun to draw the attention and arouse the efforts of many of the country's best gun makers, among whom was Matthew Browning, patriarch of the clan of gun makers still operating under that name today, whose first gun shop was located in a small Iowa town just on the fringe of the western territory. It thus may seem strange that Charles Parker had never attempted, before the years immediately preceding the war, any ventures into firearms manufacture; but if we stop for a moment to consider the industrial nature of gun making, it becomes apparent that his failure to do so was an indication of the sound judgment which had characterized his entire career and made him the most successful manufacturer in the Meriden area.

The manufacture of guns, even on a limited scale, is a complex and rather demanding project. And in the case of factory production which would have been the only type feasible for such a concern as Parker, it was even in the mid-nineteenth century a fairly large scale affair. To have engaged in any form of it as a personal venture into the field would thus have necessitated either a complete overhaul of a large portion of the company's facilities or the opening of an entirely new factory devoted to this line alone. Since Charles Parker had had no previous experience in gun making and no doubt had had no cause to acquire any revolutionary firearms patents, or any gun making what he deemed a good business prospect, he undoubtedly had never seen any reason to add firearms or any kind of weapon to his already very extensive line of products.

But, as the old cliche puts it, the war changed all that, although it was not precisely the war nor even perhaps the threat of war that precipitated Parker's first venture into gun making. It is not apparent just how the firm happened to receive its first contract for guns nor can it be accurately determined whether Charles Parker accepted the chance to make rifles for the government as simply another opportunity to add grist to his already busy mill or whether he was already thinking in terms of guns as his sole or principal future line. If the former is true, he no doubt felt that a government contract was a key to future opportunities in this field. If the latter is the explanation, then certainly the mechanical changes necessary for production of rifles on a limited and temporary scale would have been the ideal and financially safe way to make the necessary preparations for entering the gun industry. A contract would mean that all guns made would be accepted and paid for in advance, and, in the event that the future did not seem to promise success in this field as a private venture, no financial losses would be sustained. If, on the other hand, the factory seemed well adaptable to successful gunmaking, the first and most important step would have been taken with an assured profit for the venture.

However the arrangement came about, the Parker factory, under the name of Parker, Snow and Company, began the manufacture of Springfield rifles and soon developed one of the earliest repeating rifles made in this country. This latter arm was produced in 1860 as a military rifle and provides one of the many curious and almost unknown footnotes to the Civil War, a footnote involving a strange relationship between the Confederate and Union Governments and extending, in the latter case, up to the White House itself and ultimately involving the world's first international governmental organization. More will be said separately of this extraordinary part of Parker history.

With the attack on Fort Sumpter, even as with the attack on Pearl Harbor, the nation's total industrial capacity was shortly converted to wartime production and the making of guns for the armies of the Union and Confederacy. Any factory capable of being converted to arms production was eventually called on to make some kind of military weapon; so it is no more unusual that such a large scale industrial concern as Parker was given an arms contract during the Civil War than it was for two such large factories as Union Switch and Signal and Singer Sewing Machines to be engaged to make the .45 Colt Service Automatic during World War II. Rather, it seems even a bit unusual that what was then a very large industrial holding in the very heart of the New England gun-making region was not given contracts for an even larger supply of guns than was actually the case. The reason probably was that the number of guns required by the Union forces did not necessitate total conversion by private industry and that Parker's other products included many that made a contribution to, or had some relation to, the war effort.

In any case, Parker's first venture into gun making, directly augmented by the war, was quite sufficient to reveal the potential possessed by the Parker factory in this line of manufacture and may have been the determining factor in Charles Parker's post-war decision to convert eventually to sporting guns as a primary product. These army-service rifles turned out by the great Meriden concern just before and during the Civil War are thus significant as the first guns made by Parker, and, by virtue of that fact, are the immediate firearm predecessor of the Parker shotgun. And so for this reason alone they would be of interest and deserve inclusion in a book about the Parker quite apart from their individual interest as a particular type of firearm.

But they are equally or even more interesting for the latter reason than for the former. The two military rifles produced by Parker's Meriden factory for the Kentucky Militia in 1860 and then for the U.S. Government are of unique design and are, to the writer's knowledge, certainly two of the rarest and most unusual of all American army rifles. Both rifles were repeaters, and repeating rifles in the mid-nineteenth century were a new and still uncertain trend in gun design.

The first, a very unusual repeating military rifle, was one of the first examples of this type of weapon ever developed in this country. It was made for Charles Parker in one of his many Meriden plants under the name which the firm used about 1859-60 and during most of the war, Parker, Snow, Brooks and Company. It was about .50 caliber, and carried the cartridges in a tube magazine in the stock; after a shot was fired, a release lever was pressed, releasing the barrel which was then turned by hand to a point where it ejected the empty cartridge, following which another loaded one would be injected into the breech. After the receiver was again locked, another shot could be fired. This unusual and rather clumsy-sounding weapon was quickly turned into a rapid fire repeating rifle by those who got the chance to use it. It was made for and used by the North Kentucky Milita in 1860 and very shortly put into use by the military forces of that region when the Civil War began. The Confederate army soon felt its vicious and apparently unprecedented firepower and their reaction to this brought about the strange episode in national and international relations spoken of earlier.

Although actual casualties caused by the very effective Parker-made repeater are of course impossible to determine or even accurately estimate, either their number or their physical nature (perhaps the latter, considering the large caliber of the cartridge) was sufficient to cause the Confederate Government to appeal to their arch antagonist, President Abraham Lincoln, to have the rifle withdrawn from service use on the grounds that is was a barbarous weapon and its wartime usage contrary to humanitarian principles. What Mr. Lincoln's personal opinion in the question was is not a matter of any known record, but he apparently felt that the Confederate appeal was of sufficient merit to be referred to the commonly accepted supreme authority in such matters; so he referred it to the Hague International Tribunal for their decision. It would be most interesting to know what attitude the international body would have taken toward the matter, but the war ended before any decision was handed down.

The second of the two repeating rifles made by Parker

was one of the first breech-loading rifles to be produced
for the United States Government during the actual
course of the Civil War, and came out in 1864. The
Parker designers and engineers must have been firm
believers in the ballistic virtues of large caliber rifles, as
this one is about .55 caliber. Its general design resembles
very closely the Colt and Whitney models then in use.
These two makes, however, were muzzle loading percussion cap rifles, while the Parker has a distinct breech
loading and ejection mechanism created exculsively by
the Parker, Snow Company. It is also equipped with a
bayonet and cleaning rod. In view of their reaction to
Parker's earlier venture into the service rifle line, we may
certainly infer that the Confederates would not have
looked with any favor on the second and larger, and
possibly the more efficient of the two rifles. Whatever
they might have done is only a matter of speculation, as
the war ended the year after the second rifle was perfected, by which time it had not had sufficient opportunity to make whatever qualities it possessed felt by
the men in grey. At least there is no record of any comment, pro or con, on either side.

Actual production figures for the rifles made in the
Parker plants are uncertain, and, what is even more
unfortunate, there is no breakdown at all for the different models produced. From the records left by Gamaliel
F. Snow, whose position in the firm was certainly of
sufficient importance to acquaint him with the facts of
the matter, Parker made about 10,000 guns during the
Civil War. These records, however, are not so much
actual factory statistics as they are personal notes by
Mr. Snow; and it may be that he did not include the
entire record. In fact, an article by Henry P. Davis in

the *DuPont Magazine* in 1934, wherein he discusses the background of the Parker Shotgun, states that during this period the firm empolyed about 450 men and produced an average of 100 rifles a day. If Mr. Davis' figures are correct, they leave an obvious problem when compared to Mr. Snow's or in any event several unanswered questions. If by "this period" Mr. Davis means the entire span of the Civil War, and his figure of 100 rifles a day is an even approximately correct average, then surely during the four long years of bloody fighting such a large concern as Parker should have made more rifles than a number which could easily have been produced in 100 days, less than one-third of one year.

If, on the other hand, Mr. Snow's records give a substantially correct figure, then we must assume that Parker's production of Civil War rifles was sporadic and/or on an extremely reduced scale. Whatever is the answer to the question of total numbers it may, I think, be assumed that the great majority of rifles actually produced during the war period was largely made up of the standard model government Springfield. I base this assumption on the fact that the two repeating rifles originated by the Parker technicians are, as previously noted, among the rarest of all American military arms. They are, for that matter, among the rarest of all shoulder weapons produced in this country and, to the present writers knowledge, are all but unknown except to specialists in Civil War Ordnance and American military arms. Certain it is that they are absolutely first rate collector's items and that whatever gun enthusiasts are fortunate enough to own them may take pride in having something which occupies a unique place in American firearms history.

Whether the Confederate protest to Mr. Lincoln regarding the first rifle's barbaric qualities was responsible for so few being made is another unanswered question. The rifle's design was new and by then prevailing standards, somewhat radical. This, plus the difficulty of mass-scale production, must have been at least a contributing factor in the small number produced.

In regard to the question of the actual number of rifles produced during the Civil War, two books on guns and weapons which made incidental mention of Parker give some figures on this matter; but again the figures do not coincide with those given in other sources and seem, at least in the second of the two books, to be more or less conjectural. The two articles do, however, give some interesting facts on Parker's Civil War production.

The first is taken from the book *Five Centuries of Gunsmiths, Swordsmiths, and Armourers 1400-1900* and though it anticipates the discussion of the first Parker shotgun by a short space, I will quote it in full:

> Meriden, Connecticut. Charles Parker established in 1832 as manufacturer of coffee mills. About 1842 he began to make vises and other hardware. In 1860 the firm became Parker, Snow, Brooks and Co., and at the beginning of the Civil War the production of fire-arms was undertaken. Received a government contract on September 28, 1863 for 15,000 Model 1861, rifled Springfield muskets at $19.00 each, deliveries being completed. During the period 1865-68 Charles Parker was president of the Meriden Mfg. Co. In 1868 the firm of Parker Brothers was formed by Wilbur, Charles and Dexter Parker, all being sons of the founder. The first shotgun was offered in 1868 and was known as the "Parker Bros.", being a hammer gun with a lighter bolting

mechanism. The fore-end fastened to the barrels by a key through a hole in the loop. In 1879 an improved fore-end was adopted which was based upon the Deeley & Edge type. On June 1, 1934, the firm was taken over by Remington Arms. Produce the "A-1" and "Trojan" lines.

Apparently, whatever the exact figures for the army Springfield, Parker must have made between ten and twenty thousand.

The second article is taken from a work by a well-known authority on American guns. Mr. Stephan Van Rensselear, in his book *American Firearms,* makes the following brief but informative statement under Parker, Charles, Meriden, Connecticut:

> About 1868—Double barrel percussion hammer and then hammerless shotguns which from the start enjoyed an enviable reputation for quality; in fact, many sportsmen still consider "The Parker" America's best shotgun ranking with England's finest custom made guns.
>
> Reputedly made 5,000 Triplett and Scott "Kentucky" rifles for the Kentucky Home Guard.

This is the only mention the writer has come across of the actual figures for the number of repeating carbines made for the Kentucky Militia, as well as the names of the men who were apparently its inventors and/or designers. Again, it has proved impossible to check these names and figures with other sources, but the "Kentucky" repeater is obviously a gun which has not escaped notice, whatever its antecedents.

It is fortunate, however, that excellent models of both repeating rifles and the first Parker shotgun are preserved and are on exhibit in Meriden. These premier examples of the first guns made by Parker were found in the Meriden home of Wilbur Parker, grandson of Charles Parker, and father of Mr. Charles S. Parker. The discovery was made in Wilbur Parker's home on Parker Avenue after his death in 1955, at which time the three unique pieces were turned over to the Meriden Historical Society for exhibit in their Society House. The originals are still on display in Meriden.

In concluding this chapter on the activities of the Parker firm during the Civil War, I think it quite appropriate to observe that the first guns actually designed and produced by Parker as an original manufacturer of weapons were products of quality, skill, highly effective firepower, and uniquely advanced gun design. These two repeating rifles which, though almost unknown today, were of sufficient importance in their own day to demand the personal attention of President Abraham Lincoln as a question of military ethics, thus clearly and unmistakably reveal the characteristics that soon came to be, and today still are, the very identifying mark of the Parker shotgun of which they were the immediate forerunner.

CHAPTER 3

The Beginning of the Parker Shotgun

THE CIRCUMSTANCES under which the Parker shotgun had its beginning are, as indicated in the previous chapter, generally well known. The manufacture of rifles for the Union forces during the war and the limited production of the unusual Parker repeaters are established, if statistically uncertain, facts. The terminal date of the manufacture of these rifles is also certain—1865, the year of the war's end. The dates which marked the important steps in the invention and development of the Parker shotgun are all matters of record and will shortly be discussed in detail. But the exact reasons for Charles Parker's decision to begin the manufacture of sporting guns as a major addition to his line and for his choice of the double barrel shotgun as the single type to be made are somewhat unexplained and a matter of conjecture. We can at least be certain that, at the age of 59, and with forty years of steadily successful industrial development and management behind him, Charles Parker's insight into the possibilities of manufacturing had not begun to fail him; nor were they destined to do so in the future. He knew a good thing when he saw it and he knew when a good thing was good for his company.

Yet, why he should have chosen the double barrel sporting gun as his premier product of the future is a question that is really a bit difficult to answer despite the fact that several answers seem to suggest themselves. He had made rifles on a limited mass-production basis for the government, but the making of quality sporting guns requires a production system precisely the opposite from that required by the mass producing of military arms. His own factory had produced two unique and excellent repeating rifles which had by no means gone unnoticed. But these two products were questionable as acceptable war weapons and perhaps ever more so for peacetime usage. The western frontier was on the threshold of its golden age in which guns would have a major share. Yet, the type of gun which was evidently in Parker's mind at the war's end was neither the type nor the quality for sale and use on the frontier even on a limited scale.

All of the above facts and contrasts would seem to suggest that some improved design of rifle would have been a more logical and plausible choice for consideration as the gun to be made by Charles Parker. But he chose the traditional if rather financially circumscribed double barrel shotgun, and perhaps it is in this very fact that the key to his choice lies. The general design and shooting qualities of the double gun, plus the particular characteristics that have always made it a top favorite, were well established in 1865. They had, in fact, been so for more than a century, since the gunsmiths of eighteenth century England had perfected the design and made it the world's top favorite sporting gun. Thus, there could be no doubt about the general acceptability of the theory of the design. In practice, improvements could, and would be made. But the basic theory of general design on which he would work was traditional; so once again, Charles Parker *knew* what was best for his factory and knew it by the best of all criteria of judgment: hindsight.

It is well to recall here that among all of the multitude of products made by the Parker factories there was none which might be seriously called an innovation, much less a novelty. His line was always distinguished by quality and sound judgment rather than new or daring experiments. To be sure, his two repeating rifles fell into this latter category; and, no doubt for that very reason, he decided not to push them farther than the stage of first level acceptance which they had received during the war. He might well have abandoned altogether the idea of further production of guns. The machinery he had used in wartime production of rifles would not begin to take care of the type of guns he intended to make. Vast re-tooling would be necessary. What, then, other than the double gun's traditional popularity really determined Charles Parker to make it? Was he personally a gun enthusiast and an admirer of the double gun in particular and did this impel him to want to make one in his own factory that would be the best in its field?

From surviving sources of information, this is the most likely explanation. From statements made by former Parker employees and their relatives and associates, Charles Parker had indeed always wanted to build a fine shotgun and at the war's close set out to secure the craftsmen to help him succeed in so doing. He was then, these reports say, urgently in need of expert gunsmiths to form a hard core of craftsmen with which to build fine guns as a specialty. Where Parker derived this interest in shotguns as such is not so precisely apparent. But it is not very difficult to make a deduction. He was mechanically-minded and had spent his whole life in the manufacturing field; he had further spent his life in the area where nearly all guns made in the country originated; as previously noted, he could not have been oblivious to trends in this field. Perhaps a personal interest in guns and more especially shotguns combined with these two factors to generate the desire to produce the very best product of this kind to be made in the United States.

It may be that, in addition, he realized that the double barrel shotgun, already an established favorite as a muzzle loader for a century, was susceptible of definite improvement on its traditional design, whereas such ideas as repeating rifles were as yet a very uncertain prospect. This fact, plus the experience in the general practice of gun making his factory had had in the war, were probably sufficient to determine Meriden's best-known industrialist, now approaching sixty, to launch his mighty holdings in the making of a new but thoroughly accepted product—the double barrel sporting gun; and this he did, in the same year the Civil War ended, 1865.

By that year, as we have previously seen, the name of the firm had again been changed, and it was known as The Meriden Manufacturing Company. It was still making the large variety of articles that Parker's catalogs had listed for many years, and had Charles Parker as its President, and, we may be sure, its dominating and guiding force. The first Parker shotgun, illustrated on the frontispiece, was developed about this same time and may have been actually completed in 1865. The exact date on which the first Parker was perfected in its final form is uncertain, but can be fixed somewhere within the limits of the years 1865-1868. In any case, it was in the latter year that the first Parker shotgun was factory made and sold under the name which the firm acquired in this same year and under which its guns have been sold ever since, Parker Brothers.

At the time of this change in name and actual ownership, the Snow family was, it will be remembered, in partial control and ownership of the factory and business holdings. But as earlier mentioned, they were shortly eliminated from the scene altogether and it was thus voted to sell the business. John Parker, Charles' brother, here appears for the first time in the story as he was given the job of selling the business and arranging its disposition. He very quickly did so, to his brother Charles, who then became owner as well as administrative director of the entire enterprise, probably to no one's surprise, least of all his own. It is here that the name Parker Brothers, which was used as the trade name for the shotgun to the end of its days, enters the picture.

It is somewhat more accurate in its connotations than the many other names the firm had used, since it did at least suggest that the business was now exclusively in the hands of the Parker family; and so it was, and within the family circle, in the hands of the one who had in fact dominated the area's and the company's policies for forty years. The Company was thus the Charles Parker Company regardless of the trade name and remained under his control and direction for some thirty-three years longer, until his death after the turn of the century at the age of about ninety-three.

It was in 1868, when the first Parker shotguns went on sale, that the company began to slowly discontinue many of its former lines. In years to come, a great number of products were dropped from the Parker catalogs, and some were also added and at the same time the gun business was sold to Remington in 1934 the company still made an impressively large line of modern home and industrial equipment. During the years following the introduction of the shotgun the factory was still especially noted for several other products. The famous Campbell Printing Press, well known in those days for the printing of country newspapers, was made there and continued in the Parker line until the late 1870's. There was also produced during this time a large variety of top-quality machines, prominent among which were sewing machines and drill presses.

The apparent lag of about three years between the time when the first Parker shotgun was completed at the factory and the time when it was produced by regular methods and released for sale can probably be explained largely by the necessity of adapting much of the factory's older machinery to the new product as well as obtaining and installing much that was entirely new. It is not to be expected that a product which, in addition to being a new and completely different addition to a factory's line, is also one of the most difficult in its own class to manufacture to high standards, could be perfected to the production stage overnight.

At this point it is well to stop for a moment to remember that, of all sporting guns ever devised by man's inventiveness, the ordinary double barrel shotgun is the one most expensive, complicated, and generally difficult to manufacture in a truly high quality model. This was true in the case of the exquisite gilded and engraved flint-lock guns used by Kings George II and III in Wind-

sor forest and by the tragic Louis XVI in the woods of
Versailles; and it is just as true in the case of the beautiful modern weapons still being turned out by Purdey,
Churchill, Lancaster, etc. in London today. It is then
quite possible that, after the completed pilot model of
the first Parker was turned out, certain difficulties developed when the factory engineers attempted to put
it into the machine stage. This would normally be true
of most new model guns even today; it would be even
more true of the effort to get a first quality double gun
out in 1865. And it was the quality which may well have
been the determining factor in the delay in getting the
Parker on the market. Several times during the history
of the gun occasions arose when certain changes or modifications in the production methods would have been
necessary if certain trends in gun production in the
United States were to be followed, trends which would
have been of possible financial advantage to the company. But in each of these cases, several of which will be
disclosed later in this book, a compromise with traditional Parker quality would have been necessary; and
whenever *any* question of that nature arose, from the
time the first Parker was completed, there was but one
answer given. This demand and search for quality and
perfection, from the very beginning of gun production,
followed without deviation from the first Parker to the
last, could have easily been of importance equal to that
of new machinery requirements *per se* in the three years
tooling up stage necessary for turning out a shotgun
which satisfied Charles Parker and his staff.

Whatever the production problems, of machinery, of
design, or of a combination of both, the Parker gun factory had solved them by 1868, the year when the first

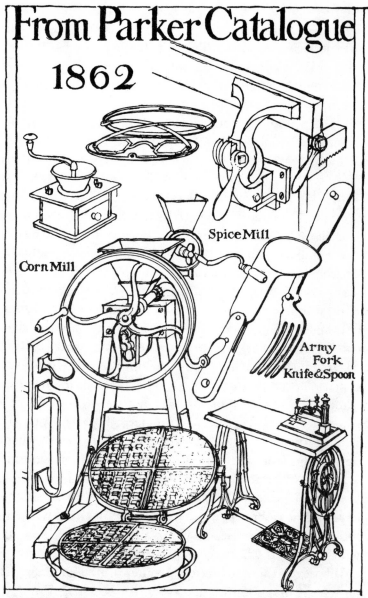

From Parker Catalogue
1862

Spice Mill

Corn Mill

Army
Fork
Knife & Spoon

Products of The Parker Company which were illustrated in the 1870 catalog.

Parker Brothers shotgun was placed on the market. This first Parker gun is naturally of much interest both intrinsically and historically, and therefore deserves detailed study and comment. It is, of course, a hammer gun, which is operated by a lifter bolting mechanism, and a fore-end fastened to the barrel by a key through a hole in the loop. It is .14 gauge with a 29 inch barrel. The old elevator type of lock was in general use at the time and shows no noticeable deviation from the standard gun lock in use on breech-loading double guns in the late 1860's. This bolting device is crude and of a very gawky and ungainly appearance, as the photograph of the first Parker reveals. But I think we may be sure that whatever its aesthetic qualities, its mechanical standard was above reproach.

The success which the Parker gun quickly achieved is, in fact, very definite testimony to that effect. The history of the Parker shows, furthermore, that this first bolting device which the gun employed must have been of sufficient appeal to the shooting public to gain an enduring place in its favor. This is evidenced by the fact that the device for bolting and opening the breech of the first Parker shotgun, a device carefully worked out by the factory's technicians, was still in use more than *thirty years* later, as will become apparent when we consider the gun's mechanism in the year 1899. All relevant facts considered, this is really astonishing. The Parker factory had, in compliance with the wishes of its founder, created a new and distinctive feature for its first shotgun. The lifter mechanism was not merely a novelty, but an improvement over all sporting guns then in use. Such an improvement was it, and so quickly did it win the confidence of the sportsmen, that it remained a standard factory design beyond the invention of not only the top-lever bolting device but even beyond the advent of hammerless shotguns.

And the reason for this success is obvious. The bolting mechanism actuated by the under-lever release was of such strength and unfailing reliability that it immediately established one of the features by which the Parker was to become best known, for which in fact it became proverbial: an absolutely tight, never failing and perfectly operating breech.

The very first Parker shotgun was thus marked by what soon came to be distinguishing characteristics of the company's entire line: creative inventiveness which made a substantial addition to the field of gun design; long-lasting value which outlived much more modern changes; and certain qualities which became, and still are, synonymous with the name Parker.

The loads used in the first Parker shotguns were of a type which formed a transitional stage between muzzle loading components and one-piece primed shells. From the beginning of firearms use, the loading components have remained a basic four: the powder which acts as propellant; the priming compound used to explode the powder; the projectile, or as in the shotgun, a group of projectiles of the same size; and whatever wadding or packing material is necessary to secure the components tightly in the bore, or the shell casing. The double barrel muzzle loader had begun as a flint-lock arm, continued with the percusion cap-and-ball mechanism when that was developed, and with the advent of breech-loading devices and more practical load combinations, had become one of the first firearms to convert to the latter improvements.

One interesting and significant point in connection with the early association of breech-loading devices and the double gun is the fact that in the United States, for many years past, and today in many parts of Europe, a double gun is often referred to as "a breech loader". The use of this term as a synonym for a double barrel shotgun, coming from a traditional popular usage, indicates what is undoubtedly an historical fact: the double gun was the first sporting gun to be produced in large quantities which made use of this outstanding improvement in gun design.

Breech-loading systems of varing kinds had, of course, antedated the development of the modern one-piece cartridge case. There are breech-loading muskets which go back as far as the 1700's. The design of the double gun, in general, probably evoked some of the earliest effort in this direction, so that by the time Parker produced its first shotgun, the breech-loading mechanism was taken for granted as standard on this type of gun. Improvements in the design of shotgun shells had been quite as rapid as in the case of rifle cartridges; so that by the time Parker took up the manufacture of sporting guns a shell was in use which constitutes an intermittent stage in the history of shotgun ammunition.

It was for this type of shell that the first Parkers were chambered and designed. Such a shot shell was made of brass and loaded with powder and shot with a suitable opening in the base for the ignition spark to reach the powder. These guns were made with nipples under the outside hammers so that, after the shells were inserted, percussion caps were placed on the nipples. The hammers and locks were of the conventional designs used as long as hammer doubles were manufactured.

From this type of shell, which eliminated the muzzle loading of components but retained the percussion cap, it was only a step to the pin-fire shell using a pin in the shell head struck by the hammer to detonate the charge, and from there to the percussion primer system which is in universal use today. This final stage in the basic development of case and primer design for shells and cartridges was reached in the early 1870's, in time for the improvement and development of the Parker shotgun, a very important stage in the gun's history and one which will be taken up in the next chapter.

CHAPTER 4

Improvement and Development

ONCE THE Parker shotgun had been finally developed to the factory-production stage and put on the public market, the next factor in deciding its future would naturally be the extent of its sale, *ie.*, its financial success. Unfortunately, no records exist of sale figures for the gun's earliest years, but there are two facts immediately apparent that give a fairly conclusive answer to the question, "Was it generally a success?". The first of these is the fact that it stayed on the market for six years; and the second that, at the end of that time, steps were taken to improve it to the point of ultimate perfection. These circumstances leave little doubt that, again, Charles Parker's foresight and methods had not gone astray. In fact, they not only leave no doubt of that conclusion, but they definitely suggest that the success of the first Parker had been such that he was fully aware that, with improvements, the gun had an even brighter future.

And small wonder that anyone with any knowledge of the gun market, much less that of old C.P., would reach this conclusion. The early 1870's saw the largest number of outstanding new gun designs that any era in the nation's history had seen so far. Through 1869-71 Smith and Wesson brought out their three superb single-action revolvers, the American, the Russian and the

45

Schofield. In the last of those three years Colt brought out what is certainly the most famous, sought-after, and romantically praised revolver of all time, the single action Frontier. In 1873 Winchester brought out the repeating rifle that would lead all rifle sales in the nation for the next twenty years and become the predecessor of the particular mechanism that is still one of the mainstays of the factory, the Model 73 lever action repeater. Marlin was likewise experimenting with the lever action design and all over New England new factories were appearing to manufacture pistols, rifles, and double and single barrel shotguns.

The Parker mechanism was a good one but rapid advancement in gun design of every type and improvement in the making of shotgun shells had rendered it obsolete. To insure the success of the Parker gun and make it a first-rank product a first-rank gun specialist, an engineer, was needed. When, after the Civil War, Mr. Parker had decided to go into the sporting guns business and planned to use the same machinery he had used during the war, he discovered that he nevertheless had to get a great deal of new machinery and even design and make some special machines. This must have been a large task, but it was one he undertook with the success witnessed by the development and six year career of his first shotgun.

When he became aware that a full-time, top-rank gun designer was necessary for the future of his gun, he set out to find him, and, once again, was successful to the point of perfection. Just how Charles Parker found the one man he needed, what standards of judgment he used in selecting him, whether his choice had previously distinguished himself by any particular achievement in gun making, are all unanswerable questions, but find him he did, in another New England city famed for gun making. In 1874, Charles A. King joined the Parker Company, coming from what was even then one of the nation's foremost gun makers, Smith and Wesson of Springfield, Massachusetts. Mr. King was largely responsible for the mechanical development of the early Parker guns, and many of the gun's patented features were invented by him. His son, Walter, followed in his father's footsteps, as did so many of the children of Parker craftsmen, and, in 1934, when the firm was absorbed by Remington, was still connected with it in an important capacity.

Mr. King, after joining Parker, developed, in succession, other lifter-type actions, bolt action hammer guns, hammerless guns (meaning here guns with inside hammers controlled by outside cocking levers), genuine hammerless guns, and then hammerless guns with automatic ejectors. But of all features of the Parker gun to be developed either in the formative years or later, the one destined to have the most enduring importance and the greatest influence on the gun's future was its bolting system. This vital part of the mechanism, perfected about 1880, is worthy of detailed analysis and description:

When C. A. King set out to re-design the bolting system of the Parker, he worked in conjunction with Charles Parker himself. This indicates either that the president of the factory was personally interested in his new product (certainly a logical possibility), or that his knowledge of mechanical devices in general was of sufficient scope to transcend any particular product, ie. a gun as a gun, and to visualize a better-made shotgun just as much as a better-made coffee mill. In any event, he and Mr. King were not satisfied with any of the current systems in use for making double guns. And here it should be remembered that this particular type of gun was entering its golden age. Colt was designing a beautiful double gun of superior quality, although it was not destined to last. The other great American makers of doubles were getting started at and around this time, Fox, Ithaca, L. C. Smith, Lefever. In addition, several outstanding systems for gun bolting, patented and used by double makers in this country and England, were quite popular and continued in use up to and beyond World War II. These were the Anson and Dealy, the Dealy and Edge and the rotary bolt, the last-mentioned continuing as long as L. C. Smith was in business, to about 1950.

But Messrs. Parker and King were not satisfied with any of these, and so they designed the Parker bolting system, which, once more, was an outstanding success for its entrepreneur; so much so, in fact, that it was never changed in principle throughout the remaining seventy odd years the gun was on the market, although as the years passed the system was improved from time to time. In its final form it operated as follows: at the rear bottom end of the barrel lug was inserted a hardened steel piece known as a combination bolt plate, into which the bolt was actuated by the top lever; this plate had a lapped surface in the center sloped at an angle of $12\frac{1}{2}°$ while the center of the bolt had a corresponding surface. On each side of this sloping part were two flat surfaces on both the combination bolt plate and the bolt which cleared each other by .005 of an inch when the gun was closed. Should the gun tend to blow open, then these two flat surfaces would prevent it. However, the bolt would never stick or jam in opening the gun due to the 12½° angle on the tapered part of the bolt and bolt plate. The degree of the angle on the complimentary tapered parts of this bolt and bolt plate was thus the most important part of the bolting mechanism.

In addition to the excellent bolt device, the gun lug had a cam shaped hook which fitted into a similar cam in the frame. These parts were scope-fitted with the absolute minimum of clearance. When the gun was fired, these surfaces locked together and thus were so effective that any Parker gun could be fired with the bolt itself completely disengaged and still not come open.

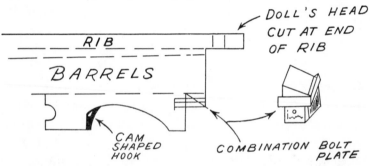

The first step in the perfection of this splendid design came about 1880, with the creation of the improved fore-end lock, achieved by means of the lug device mentioned above. It was based on the Dealy and Edge system. The last was taken in 1910 when the combination bolt plate was given the form it took for the remainder of the gun's existence.

A word is in order here about the materials used for making the barrels of the early Parkers and the improvement and development these materials underwent in later years. This is important not only as an aspect of the gun's intrinsic quality but as the criterion of difference among the early models. The latter circumstance came about through the system of Parker grading. In the earliest years of the gun's history a hierarchy of grades was set up to designate the different qualities of workmanship put into the gun on an ascending scale. This discrimination between grades, based on the amount and type of work done on each grade, and adopted fairly soon after the gun's development, probably about 1872, remained the guide to the general production of the Parker line until the company went out of business. In the years during and after the first World War, grading was done on a basis of both the amount of general workmanship and the type of steel used in the barrel.

In the early models of the Parker, however, grading was based entirely on the type of figured steel used in the gun's barrel. This factor involves one of the most frequently encountered aspects of gun making in past generations and one which is still something of a problem to the every-day user of the shotgun—Damascus steel barrels. Because of the facts that shotgun shell boxes still carry warnings against the use of smokeless-powder shells in guns with Damascus or twist steel barrels and one occasionally hears of someone being injured by such a gun blowing up, many persons are under the impression that steel of this type is of a poor, inferior and dangerous quality. But this is most definitely in error. In fact, precisely the opposite is true of Damascus steel. Barrels made of it were usually of the finest quality possible to make, and capable of the most exquisite workmanship. It was from the beautiful designs often used to decorate them that the term "Damascus", sug-

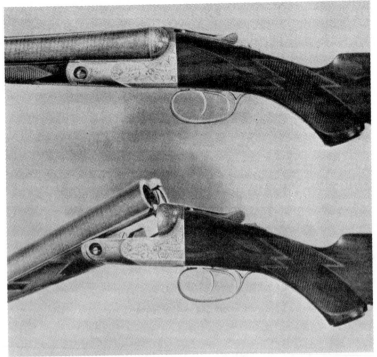

C. H. Grade to meet "the demand for a medium-priced, artistic, handsome and durable gun." The barrels were of fine Damascus steel finely figured or Acme steel of high grade without figure.

gesting oriental craftsmanship, is derived. But, of course, such barrels were made at a time when smokeless powder, with its increased pressures, had not been developed, and were thus not intended for shells loaded with it. These barrels make quite a chapter in the history of shotguns, actually an integral part of their history and the craftsmanship involved is worthy of serious study in itself.

These so-called Damascus barrels were made by winding alternate strands of wrought iron and steel wires around each other to form a cable. This cable was then wound around a mandril and welded in a furnace.

steel in layers, according to the figures that may be desired. These layers are securely welded together into a compact bar, as shown in Fig. 1, which must be absolutely sound and perfect in every weld, as the slightest spot left unwelded or unsound in this operation will be sure to cause a total loss of the barrel. The process now consists in reducing this bar to such a sized rod as may be required for a certain weight of barrel. This rod is now twisted similar to a rope, as shown at E in Fig. 2, care being taken to have the twist uniform and even. Several of these twisted rods are now placed side by side, being careful to have the inclination of the twist arranged in opposite directions, as shown in the illustrations. These several rods are now welded together with the same care and precision as in the previous operation, to insure perfectly sound barrels. This is now termed a ribbon and is coiled spirally around a mandrel, as shown at F in Fig. 2. This spiral ribbon is now raised to a welding heat and jumped by striking the end against the anvil, thereby welding the edges firmly together. They are then placed upon a welding mandrel, reheated, and welded from end to end. Much skill and care is required in this operation to reduce the outside diameter to correct size and at the same time preserve the calibre, and also maintain the proper taper, the barrel being much larger at the breech than at the muzzle. The fine figure that appears in the figured barrel is dependent upon the correctness of this and the previous welding operations, for if hammered unevenly, the figure itself will be correspondingly uneven. Then follows the process of hammering in nearly a cold state, whereby the texture of the metal is condensed, closing its pores and making it harder. This finishes the operation of barrel-forging, and the barrel is now ready to be bored, turned and finished upon lathes manufactured expressly for the purpose. The curly figure that appears in the Damascus, Bernard and Laminated barrels, as shown at G in Fig. 2, is obtained by twisting the rods before refered to, as appears in the illustration at E in Fig. 2, the variation of figure being obtained by varying the piling. The white marks that appear in the finished barrel are iron and the dark ones the steel. The fine figure that is on the barrels of the high-priced guns is obtained by an increased number of pieces in the operation of piling. This larger number of pieces necessarily renders the operations of securing perfect welding much more difficult, and the liability of losses greater. Some people imagine that the curly figures of the barrels are

Method of making Damascus barrel.

When a cut was taken on these barrels and then the barrel etched (blued) with certain acids, the effect of the acid was different on the steel from what it was on the wrought iron. This difference created the so-called figure of the barrel. Early Parker guns were graded as follows (before the introduction of automatic ejectors):

PH.   The gun with so-called "plain twist" barrel.
GH.   The gun with 2, blade, Damascus barrels (meaning two curls per lap of the cable on the mandril).
DH.   Three blade barrels.
CH.   The gun with Bernard twist barrels (a very fancy barrel and Parker's best gun).

All of these barrels and tubes used by the Parker were made in and around Liege, Belgium. So far as the knowledge of still-living Parker officials goes, none were ever successfully made in the United States. These barrels, which were imported as "rough tubes," with a low tariff were reasonable in price and very beautiful; but with the advent of progressive burning powder after World War I they were doomed as they were unsafe to use with these new and more powerful powders. So at that time Parker Brothers, certainly not to be left behind by such a plain and inescapable necessity, discontinued the use of them and started making their own barrels from the latest American steel that had been developed during World War I. It is interesting but hardly surprising to note that when Parker changed from figured barrels to those made of fluid steel the factory officials destroyed under a hammer all the barrels that they still had in their inventory rather than run the risk of these barrels ever being used.

The development of progressive burning powder,

mentioned in the previous paragraph, had an effect on the design as well as the material used in Parker barrels. As this new powder was developed, it was found necessary to change the shape of the gun barrels. The old Damascus barrels were thick at the breech and curved in quickly and gracefully ("swamped in" was the phrase used to describe the shape). The new barrels had a much straighter taper, the purpose of which was to give more thickness six or eight inches down the barrel from the breech. This is the approximate point at which shells loaded with progressive burning powder exert their maximum pressure as compared with the old shells loaded with black and dense smokeless powder, whose maximum pressure was delivered about two inches from the breech while the powder was still in the shell itself.

And so having considered the outstanding points in the improvement and development of two of the three principal parts of the Parker (and any double-barrel gun), the bolt and the barrels, we may leave the stock to be considered in the chapter on the actual technique of producing the gun and now devote a very brief chapter to the outstanding dates in Parker's total history and the additions and other improvements marked by these dates.

CHAPTER 5

Outstanding Dates In Parker History

I HAVE, particularly in the previous chapter, considered in detail only the outstanding developments in the history of the Parker Company in general and its famous shotgun in particular. In the case of the company, only as much detail and information are necessary as to form the background and origin of Charles Parker's extensive manufacturing interests, specifically as these interests first became involved with gun making and from there went into the building of shotguns. In the case of the gun itself, I have been as detailed as my sources of information and facts so far available permit; and these, not surprisingly, have been chiefly concerned with such outstanding landmarks in the gun's history as the bolting system, the barrels, and, antedating these, the first contact Parker experienced with gun making.

But this does not imply that Parker's history shows only a few important dates. On the contrary, the century-long span which this book covers would, if thoroughly analyzed, reveal an almost continuous stream of successes, additions, modifications, and deletions, each marking some form of improvement in either gun or company or both. Many of these items would be beyond the scope of this book or only indirectly related to it. Others, while germane to the subject, would not be of such a nature as to be worthy of detailed analysis. However, I think a chronological listing of the outstanding dates in the history of the Charles Parker Company and what they signify well worth making. Set down specifically in relation to the history of the Parker Gun, these dates and their importance bring before us more than a century of steady progress and industrial advancement, an unfailing foresight and ability to discern mechanical trends, a willingness to follow every new mechanical and scientific improvement in the realm of firearms, a willingness to follow as well, where practicable, public preferences in gun design, and above all an absolute refusal to ever compromise quality with sales potential.

In a period of more than a century, these dates may seem comparatively few even if they are all considered outstanding. To be sure they do reveal the progress of a company almost entirely devoted to one type of gun, one whose policy was always cautious and essentially conservative, and one which was slow to make changes until such changes were demanded by scientific advancement or the company's own experimental research. But they also reveal a straight-forwardness and integrity of purpose and policy that must evoke respect and admiration.

> 1828.   Charles Parker goes into business with blind horse and one-room power plant.
>
> 1832.   Charles Parker founds the Parker Company whose business is the manufacture of coffee mills.
>
> 1842.   Company begins to make and sell vises.
>
> 1860.   The firm becomes known as Parker, Snow, Brooks and Company.
>
> 1859-60. Company begins the manufacture of guns with the 50 caliber repeating carbine for the Kentucky Militia.

1862.   Catalog for entire concern lists several hundred items.

1861-65. Company makes Springfield rifles for the government on contract.

1864.   Company develops second repeating carbine, of 55 caliber.

1865.   Company takes the name of Meriden Manufacturing Company with Charles Parker as president.
          Charles Parker decides to go into the manufacture of sporting guns.
          First Parker Shotgun developed.

1868.   Company again reorganized under the name of Parker Brothers.
          First shotguns made by factory methods and put on the market.

1874.   Charles A. King, father of the Parker Gun, joins Parker after coming from Smith and Wesson.

1880.   Fore-end lock developed, used to the end of the company's existence on all but the lowest priced guns.

1882.   The use of a sliding lifter bar in front of the trigger guard to operate bolting mechanism discarded in favor of a top-lever action which made use of an auxiliary roundbolt and a bolt lever pivoted beneath the tang.

1889.   Adoption of a hammerless type of lock mechanism, the most radical change up to that time.

1902.   Design and incorporation of an automatic ejector, essentially unchanged in years following.

1905.   First 28 gauge shotgun perfected and produced by Parker.

These two prints represent a high point in Parker history, the transition stage from hammer to hammerless mechanism. The pictures were on correspondence envelopes, the upper dated 1887, the lower 1889. Prints courtesy of *The Gun Report*.

1910. Perfection of traditional Parker bolt by combination bolt feature.
Improvement of top lever action.

1915. Parker Trojan, first economy grade gun produced by Parker, offered.

1916-17. Cocking mechanism radically altered by James P. Hayes, reducing number of parts from 18 to 4.

1917. First single barrel shotgun produced, designed for trap shooting.
Flat top-lever spring discarded in favor of coil type.

1919. Outstanding year for scores made with Parker guns. Winnings, perfect scores and records made this year too numerous to mention. Parker Gun maintains its reputation of being the best shooting gun in the world.

1920. Fred Gilbert, of Spirit Lake, Iowa, demonstrates shooting qualities of the Parker by scoring 589 straight in a competition. 589 without a miss was then the *World's Record.*

1922. Single trigger put into production for Parker guns.

1923. First Beavertail fore-end perfected and introduced by Parker.

1926. First ventilated rib, adopted to the double barrel gun, offered by Parker.

1927. First Parkers in .410 gauge produced.

1928. Production figures reach 190,000.

1930. Production of 200,000th Parker celebrated by creation of Parker Invincible Grade, the most luxurious and expensive sporting gun ever produced in North America and probably the most luxurious and expensive conventional sporting weapon produced to that time in the Western

Hemisphere. Only two Invincibles produced, first one with the serial number 200,000.

1934.   On June 1st, Remington Arms Company assumes control of Parker. Factory remains at Meriden for present. No changes made in production.

1934-37.   Manufacture of Parker Gun continued at Meriden. By end of 1937 manufacture is terminated by Remington. Some parts sold to Lefever Gun Company of Frankfort, New York, some disposed of locally. Transfer of business to Ilion, New York begins. Majority of Parker employees, including all skilled craftsmen, go to Ilion. Machinery for gun making moved also.

1937.   Part of factory at Ilion ready to resume manufacture of Parker. Last Parker Catalog issued.

1938.   Manufacture of full Parker line resumed at Ilion factory.

1940.   February 16th—Last Parker Jobber's Price List issued.

1941.   Last year of any quantity production.

1942-44.   Parkers made on extremely small scale during war years.

Some assembled from parts already produced before beginning of war.

1945-47.   Last Parkers made. Production largely from tag ends or only paper transactions. Possibly a new gun at times by special order.

1947.   Last Parker shotgun, either made or assembled, leaves Ilion factory. No record of whether gun was an actual production or an inventory gun, or of any of the specifications.

CHAPTER 6

Special Features Of The Parker

IN CONSIDERATION of any firearm of superior quality, it is naturally to be taken for granted that such an arm embodies certain special or even unique features. Superiority in mechanical design, after all, not to say top-rank status, is not achieved by the product's merely being a "good one" in its class. And so it is that the Parker, the country's outstanding shotgun, presented several features quite different from other double guns, features which were a material contribution to its quality and reputation for reliability and which are therefore deserving of special treatment in a chapter to themselves. One of these, perhaps the gun's outstanding mechanical aspect, was certainly its superb bolting mechanism. This has been discussed in a description of the gun's general development, since work on the bolt system constituted the very first effort by Charles Parker and Mr. C. A. King to evolve a signal improvement in the gun's design after its first few years on the market. The evolution of the bolting system, though slow like all Parker developments, was, also like all Parker developments, sure, steady, and successful.

In this connection, it must surely have become apparent by this time that the policy of the Parker factory from the time it began to manufacture shotguns could be best characterized as ultra-conservative. This is revealed by the concentration on one product, the time taken to develop new aspects of design, and the refusal to modify the company's line merely to create greater sales returns.

Major Charles Askins, in his two very practical and informative books, *The American Shotgun* and *Modern Shotguns and Loads,* speaks of the Parker in a most complimentary manner. In the former, published in 1910, he remarks that the more moderately priced Parkers are "perfectly balanced" guns, and that they shoot as well as any gun on the market. In the latter book, published in 1931, he remarks that the Parker Company is certainly the most conservative gun builder in the United States, if not in the world. He gives as the cause of this the fact that Parker, after all, has always known when it had a good feature and has generally seen no reason to be in a hurry to drop a good thing. One thing which Major Askins thought worthy of note was that the "Parker of today (meaning 1930), looks a great deal like the Parker of fifty years ago."

It is true that the changes in the Parker, especially external ones, were slow and far between, and that this fact is testimony to the skill of the factory's technicians, just as much, actually, as the fact that the external design of the Mauser Military Automatic Pistols never being changed in the near half century it was made, is a tribute to the skill—nay, the genius—of Wilhelm Mauser.

The outstanding features of any gun are best seen and understood in a description of the actual building of the gun. A lengthy and detailed chapter will be devoted to the building of the Parker; but, because of the unique mechanical and artistic nature of several aspects of this process, it seems desirable to discuss these particular aspects out of turn in the present chapter.

When one speaks of the "special features" of the Parker, the phrase immediately denotes, to anyone who has ever been fortunate enough to handle one, two not merely special but outstanding features: the balance and the closing of the breech. These features, properly considered, are of course the result of design and mechanical perfection, rather than original qualities, and so may be very logically considered apart from the actual building of the gun. When anyone who has the slightest knowledge of the use or handling of guns casually picks up a Parker, the immediate reaction is: "Wow! how that thing handles," or "say, the way she comes up!"

Just before the start of this book, I had the pleasure and pride of showing my own Parkers to a friend and former student. The man, a Naval officer from South Carolina, who was reared in the state's best hunting country and who had hunted with repeaters since he was fourteen, was anxious to see my Parkers. He had heard me brag about them, and having almost no experience even in the handling of double guns, was curious about a weapon which could evoke such enthusiasm on the part of its owner. When I removed the gun from its trunk case, snapped it together in ten seconds and handed it to him, he lifted it slightly, then, as if by natural muscular reflex, brought it to his shoulder. He then remarked: "Oh boy, I never knew a gun could have balance like that. It comes up almost automatically, like it was moving itself instead of me doing the lifting. I never had any idea they made a gun with such class in the U.S."

The Commander's reaction is typical of the reaction

shown by those who handle a Parker for the first time. It is also, unfortunately, a revelation of the sad but quite prevalent fact that this generation of Americans is almost completely unaware of the fact that high grade double guns of superb artistry and mechanical skill were turned out by American gun makers for more than half a century. The mass production mania in even art itself has sufficiently curtained America's heritage of skill in craftsmanship so that the present age is hardly aware that such talent ever existed in our country.

The phrase used by the Commander as he handled the Parker, describing how it comes up to the shoulder "like it was moving itself instead of me doing the lifting," is eloquent testimony to the superb balance of the Parker. Another sportsman whom I once knew, a double enthusiast, once remarked: "For a man to really enjoy shooting a shotgun, it's got to be really special. In fact, a shotgun, if it's a *good* one, is something that *comes alive* in your hands." The Parker, of all shotguns, lives up to this requirement uniquely. Or if that is a statement which some might consider broad and open to question, I can only advise them to go to a large gun store and actually try a Parker in comparison with any other double, American or foreign. The results will speak for themselves.

In speaking of the closing of the breech, I am of course referring by implication to the design of the bolting mechanism. This, as previously indicated, was a part of the Parker's design which, from the beginning, received close and constant attention from the factory craftsmen. Again, as in the case of proper balance, the result of this care is more than just obvious; it is outstanding. When anyone handles a Parker, the first thing he does, as in the case of any double barrel gun, is to open the breech. The strong but smooth-working top lever, without the tiniest fraction of play in either direction, moves briskly; the barrels, if the gun is cocked, go down smoothly, or, if the hammers are down, the barrels respond to a little pressure. But when the gun is closed—then is when the user is really aware of the precision work back of the piece in his hands. A Parker snaps closed like a crisp, cold leaf of fresh lettuce responding to a knife. The click of the breech, the snapback of the top lever, these are so sure, so precise, so positive in their function that the one holding the gun knows at once that he is using the utmost it is possible to produce in a gun of this type.

It is, in fact, probably more from the bolting device than from any other feature of its design that the Parker came to be known as, "The Old Reliable." There is no feature of a double gun that is more apt to inspire confidence on first examination than the manner in which the gun closes. This is so because the first motion of the one handling it, providing of course that he has developed proper habits of gun safety, is to open the breech to make sure it is not loaded. Here, again, I would only advise anyone to make this experiment with a Parker. The psychological effect is of the same kind derived from starting the motor of a Rolls Royce or Mercedez.

In considering the specific mechanical features of the Parker, which can be classified as special, we may next mention the hammers. These were made in one piece with the firing pin as an integral part of the hammers. Hence the problem of a broken firing pin does not occur. In addition, a special rebounding mechanism was provided at the bottom of the hammers so that after the pin part of the hammer hit the shell primer it automatically withdrew out of the way and never stuck in the indentation made in the primer.

All springs in Parker guns made after about 1919 were of the coil type. No flat leaf springs were used in the late models. The most important springs were enclosed in such a way that if one should break, it would still function. This was true of the main hammer springs, ejector springs, and the top lever spring.

All gun barrels were proof tested, after all the boring cuts had been made, with specially loaded shells. These shells exerted a pressure of about nine to ten tons per square inch (the normal load exerting about four tons per square inch), after which the barrels were stamped with the Parker proof mark P.

In connection with the proving of gun barrels and the special precautions taken to prevent accidents, the Parker Company had an insurance policy with Lloyds of London protecting them from suits which would be brought against them for injuries or damages caused the shooter by burst barrels. Lloyds, as famous a name in insurance circles as Parker was among gun makers, was the only insurance company that would sell Parker Brothers such coverage. It was never called upon to pay a claim for such injuries.

In the general manufacture of the gun, no malleable iron or other type castings were used. All parts were made of steel forgings, such as the frames, top levers, fore-end irons, lugs and hammers. Although this was quite expensive and, of course, added materially to the cost, the company felt it necessary in order to give the gun its strength and durability.

The most intricate and important part of the actual mechanism of a double gun is the locks. This, involving the cocking mechanism, can literally make or break a gun. After all, a gun may have barrels of super strength, a bolting mechanism to match, and perfect balance, but if the actual mechanism for firing the load does not function properly, all the other aspects of the gun go to no real purpose.

And here Parker was not lacking any more than it had been in any other part of the gun's design. One of the early developments had been the adoption of the hammerless cocking system in 1889. Although somewhat radical at this time, the system was not by any means unknown. The Colt shotgun, first produced in 1883, had used it; and by 1889 it was very well known in England. Parker, however, had as usual been cautious and did not rush to adopt what was still a very sharp deviation from the locking system which had prevailed for more than 125 years. After the hammerless system had been devised and at such time as it had been definitely accepted by the public and, more important, when the company had devised its own system commensurate with its standards, Parker changed to the hammerless cocking design which was well enough devised to last for the next twenty-five years without major improvement.

At the end of that time an improvement was made that may indeed be termed major. Here, once again, Parker came out with a contribution to the making of double mechanisms which may fittingly be called unique. For just before World War I, one of Parker's technicians, Mr. James P. Hayes, made what is certainly the most radical change in the theory of gun cocking mechanisms ever devised. Mr. Hayes, who had devised the top lever, bolt and ejector then in use, all of which had been patented in his name, invented a new form of cocking device by which *eighteen* parts, yes *eighteen,* were reduced to *four.*

This amazing change is no doubt the one covered by the latest date stamped on Parker guns made during the company's last years. That date is October 25, 1910. Whatever the exact date on which the change was made in general factory production, it was incorporated in every gun made from that time until manufacture of the gun ceased in 1947.

The changes made in the cocking mechanism are very interesting; and in this case I am fortunate enough to have the actual words of Mr. Hayes, taken from his original statement concerning his invention. He says:

"I have discarded 18 of the original parts and have replaced them with 4 very simple pieces. The gun so remodeled cocks much smoother and easier than the regular Parker guns do.

"The unhooking mechanism is thrown out entirely. I have retained the spiral main spring, plunger, and stirrup without alteration. Below is a list of parts I have discarded. (These I have omitted)

"The hammers have 5 operations left off from them, thus making right and left hammers alike.

"The trigger plate has the head end cut off as per sketch, which makes an easy piece to fit into the frame and does away with 2 screws.

"The trigger plate being made in this form allows the frame to be shaped differently and makes the frame much stronger. The barrel lug, is the same as the hammer gun lug, thus allowing the use of the checkpin as in the regular hammer gun.

"The 18 pieces may be discarded and the 4 new

pieces put into a completed gun without having to alter the frame except to provide holes and slots for the new pieces."

When one carefully considers Mr. Hayes' description of his modification of the gun's most vital feature, it is no wonder that Parker guns are known for durability and that one never hears of a broken Parker or even of one needing actual mechanical repair.

This chapter may be fittingly concluded with a discussion, necessarily brief, of that particular feature of the Parker's exterior appearance which today is likely to invoke as much interest as any other feature of the gun, which, in fact is usually the first aspect of the gun to draw comment from an onlooker—the engraving. This appeal which a gun's appearance, and in particular whatever style and amount of engraving it happens to possess, exercise on the imagination of the observer is, of course, purely a question of aesthetic reaction and awareness of skill and craftsmanship, and these are both areas of the human psyche which have no necessary connection with technical skill. I say "no necessary connection" since it is quite true that mechanical perfection may very well appeal to the human being's artistic sense, as well as to his natural admiration for technical perfection *per se* in anything. It will, to be sure, almost inevitably do so should such a person have any degree of imagination.

But the fact is that where guns are concerned the engraving, be it the world's finest, is not an integral part of the gun's mechanical qualities and so is not an ingredient contributing either to its handling or shooting ability. Its function is purely decorative—to give the piece it adorns some special mark of quality and artistic craft, to present the part played by art as well as science. Engraving has been a part of gun making from the beginning, and is today as much honored and admired if not as much in actual demand as ever. And it seems that the demand would be as great in our own country in 1959 as it was in Europe in the earlier centuries if the average American gun lover had the means to pay for it. American in their love and admiration for fine guns, are by no means unaware of the engraver's art, and so look for examples to admire if they cannot have them made to order.

This is precisely the reason why a Parker, almost any Parker turned out, immediately draws interest and enthusiasm, for with the exception of the cheapest grade, all Parkers for almost the entire life of the company were adorned with at least token engraving. And beyond the three lowest grades, on all those carried in the catalog since 1913 the engraving is superbly beautiful. The whole question of engraving on a gun, despite its constant appeal, has led to a certain amount of misunderstanding on the part of many persons who are under the impression that the cost of a gun with beautiful engraving and wood checkering pays for these features only. Some who hold this opinion would well say that there is no more real work in a fifty dollar gun than in one costing five hundred. "It's just the extra icing on the cake," is the metaphor often used to express this idea. Well, such persons are wrong, and the chapter dealing with the production of Parker guns will explain the difference in grades.

Where Parkers are concerned, however, the very fact just mentioned, that Parker featured engraving as a part of all guns in its catalog except the strictly economy model, is another indication of the quality and distinction which marked the gun's exterior as well as its mechanism.

It is almost unnecessary to add that the engraver's art thus played a vital and permanent role in the history of the Parker factory and its employees, and that the engravers and their work constituted one of the most interesting parts of the factory scene.

The factory of course maintained its standard of engraving for the entire line on a progressive scale and on those models constituting about the first-half of the scale the designs used were standard. On fine guns, however, (and here the term "fine" was one used in the factory to designate those in the upper-half of the scale, above Grade DHE), and especially on the AAHE and Al special (the two top models in the catalog), engraving could be very much to the customer's individual taste. Often the purchasers of these grades brought in pictures of hunting scenes or of their favorite dogs which they wanted reproduced on their gun. Whenever any one of these fine guns was built, a plaster of paris impression was made of the engraving on the top sides and the trigger plate. These impressions were then kept on file for the future reference of customers who often selected the engraving for their guns by referring to the company's file of plaster casts.

In this connection, an incident once occurred at the plant which is quite illustrative of an unfortunate aspect of human nature and which at the same time reveals the integrity of the top personnel of Parker and the pride which they took in the distribution as well as the making of their guns. A very wealthy, and apparently equally haughty individual, was selecting his engraving. The file of plaster casts, which must have been quite extensive at the time, and which undoubtedly included numerous outstanding examples of the art, was yet not sufficient for this "connoisseur's" standards and taste. He expressed his displeasure by contemptuously sweeping aside the casts with the back of his hand, breaking several of them. Mr. King, the son of the father of the Parker gun who was waiting on the "gentleman," calmly picked up the pieces and then informed him that Parker Brothers did not care to sell him a gun.

There are of course several types and styles of engraving, the most difficult to produce being the heavy German type, found on such guns as the Sauer. The Parker was more of the light English scroll type. Most of this was done under a glass. Here it may be noted that engraving on steel is very difficult and requires the absolute ultimate in training and individual craftsmanship. This is true, because while engraving or chasing on silver is done by pushing the chisel or engraving tool by hand, the same process on steel requires that the implement be propelled with a hammer. The engravers at Parker were like all its other technicians, at the top of their profession and, because of the personal contact necessary in learning the art, educated their own apprentices, generally their sons. This part of the factory's work was, above all others, like an old fashioned guild system. All living employees of the firm with whom I have had contact have remarked that it was fascinating to watch the engravers working at their art.

The results of this system of training and its standards are manifest in the entire Parker line, and constitute a large part of the pride of ownership taken by anyone who is fortunate enough to own any of the higher grades.

CHAPTER 7

The Factory and its Employees

MENTION has been made already in several places of the general type of concern which Parker maintained, both in its origins, development, and after commencing the manufacture of shotguns. Enough has been said of the gun factory in particular to indicate that it was obviously, from the beginning, staffed by experts on every level, who took the utmost pride and satisfaction in their work. Just how much pride and personal interest went into the making of a Parker, any Parker, will be more fully revealed in the next chapter, in which the production process will be discussed in detail. Another fact that the history of the gun has made clear is that the Parker staff included not only men who were top-rank craftsmen and technicians in virtue of the work which they did, but some who were talented and highly versatile inventors, men who not only made but created, several of whom were responsible for additions and improvements to the Parker line which were major innovations in the entire field of double gun design.

The system of engraving and instruction given in this art certainly furnishes one of the most interesting and aesthetically satisfying aspects of the factory's organization. This system of personal instruction and association, often on a father and son basis, is one only too conspicuous by its absence from the modern industrial

73

scene. The fact was, however, that the entire factory, from office clerk through foreman and inspector to the president, was pervaded by the old fashioned *esprit de corps* which resulted from the feeling of personal pride each worker took in both his particular job and the finished product. This personal concern of every worker with the total integrity of the firm's product which was an innate part of the Parker company may well be illustrated by a tale once told by the Chairman of the Board of Rolls-Royce, makers of what that firm calls quite justifiably the best car in the world. Commenting on the personal concern of every employee with the quality of the Rolls, he stated: "It simply would not be possible for an automobile with anything wrong with it to ever be sold. The doorman wouldn't let it go out the door."

The achievements of individual members of the firm are indeed impressive, and those previously mentioned make, in themselves, a distinguished honor roll: Mr. Charles A. King's perfection of the bolting system; Mr. James P. Hayes' invention of the systems for the top lever, bolt, ejector, and locks (Mr. Hayes also designed a multiple drill press which was in use in the Parker factory long after the firm ceased manufacture of guns and which was still there as late as 1943. He also had a patent on a gauge and helped design pin machines); the quality of engraving done by, among others, Mr. William C. Liedtke, who is, at the writing of this book, 86 years old and the oldest living Parker employee.

Some of the earlier but less conspicuous achievements by individual members of the staff are certainly very interesting if not so spectacular as those mentioned above, while the work turned out by some of the employees is interesting both for its own sake and the sidelight it gives about the ones who did it.

The close connection which Parker had with U.S. arms production during the Civil War and the interesting footnote to the war itself which this connection furnished have been covered in a previous chapter. At least one other connection of Parker employees with American history of this period has come to light during the research on this book. Both this and the afore-mentioned matters are worth including in a discussion of Parker employees.

Among the master gunsmiths employed by Parker in its formative years were the Storm brothers, George and Jerome. The grandson of the former, a retired Colonel of the U.S. Army, lives in Fair Haven, Vermont.

The great-grandfather of the present Colonel Eric Foster Storm (Ret.), Anthony Storm, was born in 1796 in Harper's Ferry, Va. (now of course West Va.) and became a well-known master gunsmith of his day. His sons, George B. and Jerome Storm, were born in Martinsburg, Va. (now West Va.) where they lived for a short time. Anthony returned to Harper's Ferry with his family and it was there that the boys grew up and, under the close supervision and tutelage of their father, learned the fine art of gunsmithing while working on the famous Harper's Ferry Rifle at the United States Arsenal.

It was while the Storms were working at the U.S. Arsenal that the famous and fateful John Brown Raid occurred. On October 16, 1859, the fiery and fanatical abolitionist, with twenty-one of his followers, crossed the Potomac, captured the arsenal and its inhabitants, and took possession of the town. The capture of Brown and his followers, by a detachment of U.S. Marines under Colonel Robert E. Lee, the subsequent trial and hanging of Brown, and the part the incident played in the psychological climate leading to the Civil War, are all parts of American history and indelibly stamped on the entire era. During this time George Storm was a Lieutenant in the Virginia State Militia. Neither he nor Jerome were injured in the Harper's Ferry incident.

At the very beginning of the Civil War, in 1861, Federal troops, out of Fort Myer, Va., took the Storm

Parker Brothers at Meriden, Conn. issued a six-page two-color circular entitled, A Trip Thru Parker Brothers. The above is an illustration of the Testing Room as depicted therein.

brothers and several other key gunsmiths of the area (all Southerners) and sent them to Springfield, Massachusetts, where they were required to work on the Springfield rifle for the duration of the war.

At the war's close, when Charles Parker sought for top-rank gunsmiths to build and develop his line of fine shotguns, his search led him naturally to Springfield, where because of wartime arms production, so many master gunsmiths were gathered. It was here that Mr. Parker, as previously noted, found Mr. Charles A. King at the Smith and Wesson Plant. But Mr. Parker also went to Springfield Armory and made an offer to George and Jerome, who were to bring with them six or seven other Harper's Ferry gunsmiths, with their families, to Meriden where they would make their homes. He found them just as they were all preparing to return to Virginia.

Master gunsmith George spent the remaining years of his life with the Parker Company, and died in Meriden in 1894. Jerome Storm also remained with the company for many years. After his retirement he moved to Washington, D.C. when he was about seventy and remained there until his death. During the years with the Parker Company, George Storm taught his son Frederick the fine skills of gunsmithing, after the boy had finished his schooling at the old Meriden Academy. After the death of his father, Frederick received a contract from Parker for the production and processing of certain parts of the gun. He held the contract until a year after Parker was taken over by Remington, *i.e.*, 1935, a total of about forty-one years.

One of Frederick Storm's skilled techniques in gun making had to do with barrel production. It was another unique contribution to the craft by a member of the Parker staff, and forms still another interesting sidelight on the making up of the older model Parker.

This particular phase of barrel production involved the case hardening and coloring process. While other gun makers were blueing barrels in a solution, and coming out with a color that would rub off after a lot of use and barrels that would pit and corrode, Frederick

Storm developed a secret method to overcome these defects. By packing his barrels in bonedust and firing them
under an intense heat in a coal fired furnace, he obtained a most remarkable blue steel coloring and perfectly hardened bores. This process, which included two
other steps, died with Frederick Storm; and although
he taught several former apprentices whom he trained,
he never revealed all of his method.

His claim was that the case hardening and coloring
process, whose secret he carried to the grave, was unique
in gun history and one of the big factors that made the
Parker famous. He also had the polishing contract for
all the Parker guns and a special department for that
operation.

Frederick Storm was well-known everywhere in the
trade as a top expert and was a most remarkable and
honorable man, a true craftsman who loved the Parker
gun and all that it stood for. He was with Parker for
more than fifty years and was awarded the fifty year
employee distinction by Remington shortly before the
manufacture of the Parker ceased. At different times he
received many offers from such firms as Fox, Winchester
and Colt. He elected, however, to remain with Parker,
and established his home in the community where he
died in 1952 at the age of 86.

The entire factory, with all of its many small but
efficient operations and various kinds of workers, was
surely a fascinating panorama of all that was best in high
quality gun making. So many of the older employees
of Parker have passed away that it has proved impossible
to secure detailed information on a number of the
various phases of the factory's operation. The engraving, case hardening of the barrels, and fitting of the

locks, described earlier, give at least a very good indication of the talent, pride, and unique creative ability which played so great a part in the making of Parker guns.

A very important part of the external finish of any gun, but especially of a high quality double and one not previously discussed in connection with the Parker, is the checkering of the stock and forearm. This process requires skill and the capacity for sustained effort, qualities all the more necessary in the case of the high-grade and specially selected wood of the variety used in the stocking of Parkers. Consideration of this art of checkering involves, in the case of the Parker, a very unusual circumstance and another interesting, or in this case even imaginative, aspect of the factory and its employees. This results from the fact that for a number of years, the checkering on a large number of Parkers, including the finest built during that period, was done by a woman, and that the checkering shop was the only part of the factory, except the business office, where women and girls worked.

The career of the principal checker, as such workers were called, illustrates very well the practices of the factory in the early part of the century, the way this particular work was carried out, and another strange and fascinating footnote to history added by the Parker Gun.

Mrs. Elizabeth L. Hanson, now retired, started her career with Parker in 1908. She worked at the factory, except for a short time when production was very slow, until 1916 when she married. Even after marriage, she returned on occasion to help when the factory was rushed. In 1928, her first husband died, leaving her with two children to support; this made it necessary for her to return to work full time, after which she remained until Remington bought the business and moved the machinery to Ilion. At this time she was asked to go to Ilion with other Parker employees, but Mrs. Hanson was afraid to make what was for her a drastic move alone

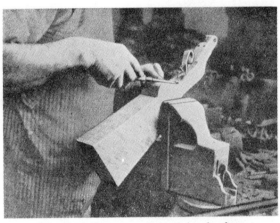

The Stock Room as pictured in circular.

and with two children. This was in 1937, so in that year ended her checkering career which, including periods of unemployment or not working because of domestic duties, had lasted nearly thirty years.

Although the job was checkering, it was commonly called checking. It was, so Mrs. Hanson says, a very hard job to learn, but anyone really interested in learning it (as she was) could do so in not too long a time. When Mrs. Hanson went to work, in 1908, there were few women in the checkering shop and only one in the factory office, although more later came to work in both sections. She started work at the age of sixteen, under the following arrangement: she would work for nothing, on a trial basis, and if she learned how to do it to the satisfaction of the foreman of this division, she would get $.50 a day for ten hours work. Mrs. Hanson spent four days working on pieces of wood, old gun stocks, and tips, at the end of which her work must have satisfied the one in charge since he put her on good work. Mrs. Hanson admits that it took her at first all day to do a tip that usually took twenty minutes, but the quality of her work and the speed with which she learned must have been exceptional. She remarks that while most of the girls that came to learn got discouraged and would not stay, she, from the beginning, always loved her work. Her career, I think, obviously makes that fact evident.

Her boss at the time she was hired and for many years afterward was Robert Rebstock, whose wife and sister-in-law also were checkers.

The work of checking, as they called it, was precise and done in the careful way with personal touches that characterized all Parker work. The boss, Mr. Rebstock, personally made all the tools used by the checkers and twice a day he would sharpen them for those who worked under him. All work to be checked was mounted in a frame and the frame fastened in a small vise on the edge of the worker's bench. The checkers used calipers and a ruler to lay out their designs on the stock, tip or butt. Some lower-priced guns, however, did not have hand-checked butts. There were just four tools needed by a checker to do a piece of work. There was a total of nine different patterns of checkering used, depending on the grade of the gun, and a different size of tool was necessary to cut out each different pattern. The higher priced the gun, the finer the checkering.

The four tools necessary for this task were as follows: the marking-out tool, which had two rows of teeth like a saw; the cutting up tool, which was V shaped, whose purpose was to cut through each mark deeply enough to eliminate shiny tops in the checkering; the tool with two rows of teeth wider apart than the marking-out tool, which was used to mark out a border all around the design; the bordering tool, with half round teeth, used to make a groove all around the border.

During the latter years of making the gun, Mrs. Hanson and the checkers used a regular engraver's gouging tool to make borders. After all the borders were cut in, the checkers would brush linseed oil over the checkering, provided there were no scratches. But if there were scratches anywhere, the boss woud remove them before he would allow oil to be put on. This is one more fine point which helps to explain the quality of the Parker. Mrs. Hanson's remark, "They were very fussy," is probably an understatement. She observes also that when she first went to work for Parker, in 1908, the company produced only eight grades of guns. This was apparently the policy from about 1900 on, and these eight grades remained the general Parker line until the last gun was made. It was during and after the first World War that the economy model and the trap and skeet guns were added. More will be said about these in the chapter on the Parker line.

That Mrs. Hanson, probably the Parker Company's outstanding woman employee, always took pride in her work, there can be no doubt. There were, however, several moments during her career when her work received recognition which made her personally very proud. These were when she was presented stocks and forearms to be checkered for guns ordered by people whose names were known the world over, and which represented the finest guns Parker turned out. Among the famous people who ordered Parkers which were checkered by Mrs. Hanson were the explorer, Bring-Em-Back-Alive Frank Buck, and the king of American movies, Clark Gable.

But of all the guns which passed across Mrs. Hanson's bench and of all those entered on the books of the Parker factory, the one which holds a truly unique place, a place not held by any other shotgun ever made in the United States, is the Parker ordered by Tsar Nicholas II of Russia. This was a magnificent weapon on which were lavished all the crafts and arts the Parker factory was at that time capable of producing. The stock, when given to Mrs. Hanson for checkering, was gold trimmed. More will be said of this Parker in the chapter on the general Parker line.

It is certainly a fact which causes one to stop and linger, however, and even to indulge in a certain amount of fanciful and nostalgic reminiscing. Tsar Nicholas, whose favorite sport and outdoor relaxation was shooting, had heard of the Parker, and despite the fact that his cousins were the kings of the two greatest gun making countries in Europe, Germany and England, and that he had quite an array of fine guns from both of these countries, he thought enough of America's finest shotgun, either through reports received of it or after handling it, to order one for himself. And of course, for the Tsar of all the Russias, it had to be the best.

It is indeed strange and ironic to think of a typical New England factory woman, a master of her trade, who had begun it at the age of sixteen, and with the typical American name of Mrs. Mike Hanson, doing a superb job of checkering on one of the finest models of America's finest shotgun; a shotgun ordered by the last head of one of Europe's oldest royal houses, and one which but for the coming of the war at the time it did, would surely have become a part of the fateful and tragic idyll of Tsarskoe Seloe, where, among the strange feats of Rasputin, the play of the stricken Tsarevich, and the carefree luxury of the Russian Empire's last days, this premier product of a Connecticut arms factory, checkered by an American woman, would have played a major role.

That the factory's outstanding checker was an American, and a woman, is a fact in which all Americans can, and all American women *should* take pride. It is to be expected, however, that a large number of the Parker employees were of foreign birth and training. This was of course due to the fact that New England, during the formative years of the Parker Company, was filled with immigrants from many nations, many of whom had had training or previous experience in either the building of guns or some form of factory work which fitted them for work at the Parker plant. Certainly the company was always interested in people who could do work meeting Parker standards, and it is a safe assumption that not an exceptionally large number of workers of any sort were capable of meeting this standard. Thus, foreign help would no doubt have been something of a necessity as well as readily available.

A breakdown of the more important specialty jobs and the nationalities of those who held them during the company's most productive years, 1900-1934, reveals the following interesting cross-section of national origin:

Forgers:	Irish
Toolmakers:	Yankees
	Swedes
Engravers:	Germans
	English
Stock fitters:	Russians from the Carpathian Mountains
Inspectors:	English
	German
Machine Operators:	Irish
	Polish

Pride of workmanship, from the beginning, played a tremendously important part in keeping up the quality of the gun. No matter how small a part any individual worker might play in the making of the gun, he took an enormous pride in seeing that the job was done properly and done well. An incident from the factory's day-to-day operation well illustrates this. In 1926, when Mr. Charles S. Parker was in charge of the shop in the absence of Mr. Walter King who was recuperating from an illness, Mr. Parker and others decided to make a minor change in the design of the frame on the DHE Grade. Accordingly, Mr. Parker wrote a notice outlining the change, gave a copy to the inspectors, and sent one to the foreman of the shop filers, a Mr. Gottlieb Anscheutz. Several days later, the inspectors reported that the change was not being made. When Mr. Parker questioned Herr Anscheutz about this fact, the latter gentleman scornfully replied, "I make them the way they ought to be." Mr. Parker, in recounting this incident, does not say whether he argued with his employee. But whether he did or not there is no doubt about whose opinion in the matter prevailed.

One of the most pleasant and appealing aspects of

the work at a factory like Parker's was the close spirit
of cooperation and pride of belonging, caused of course
by the pride of workmanship and the personal contacts
which, as indicated, played so large a part in the building of the gun. Another fact which explains why the
employees were able to always act as one big happy
family is that the number of them was never large. For
reasons which I will shortly explain, it is not truly possible to state a definite number of employees on the
payroll at any one time. It is a known fact, however,
that in the days of the Company's largest production
the number of employees in the Parker Gun Factory
did not exceed between 250 and 300, and usually the
number was much smaller.

In any event, the people who worked for Parker, like
the personnel of any old-fashioned firm where craftsmanship counted and associations were lasting, had their
traditions, customs, and moments of communal pleasure.
One matter covered by tradition was the work dress of
the employees. Mechanics and gun fitters wore dark
colored aprons, inspectors and department heads wore
white aprons, while the head inspector and foreman
of the tool room wore linen dusters. Barrel straighteners
and barrel borers wore derby hats. On the opening
day of the hunting season very few men showed up
until noon, at which hour they reported for work in
their hunting clothes and bringing any game they might
have shot during the morning. Dogs were then told to
"charge" under the workmen's bench and work proceeded.

The last working afternoon before Christmas was a
festive one indeed. Many workers brought in samples
of their homemade wine, fruitcake, cookies and other

traditional good things of the season. All invited their friends to partake. This went on until a man decided he had had enough of this sort of thing, whereupon he went merrily homeward. Everybody joined in, including the Plant Manager. A good time was had by all.

One factor which certainly was a major contribution to the overall quality of the Parker was the system of hiring in force at the factory for a number of years. That all Parker employees were outstanding, or even unique men and women in their field does not require re-emphasis here, but the conditions and terms under which they were often engaged had a definite effect on the product which they turned out.

For a long time, the old-fashioned contract system of hiring prevailed in the shop, whereby each department head was responsible for hiring and paying his own men. The company paid the department head, or contractor as he was called, a fixed amount of money for the total operations that he performed on the guns, the amount varying with the grade of the gun. For example, the office paid the engraving contractor $.90 each for the engraving on the VHE (the lowest-priced gun in the line except the economy model), and $50.00 for an A-1 special. The contractor then paid his own men either by piece work or by the day and if he could make a good profit for himself by the way he managed the transaction, that was entirely agreeable to the company directors.

From the standpoint of the company, this was a very good arrangement because it made it possible for the office to always know production costs very accurately, and not to have too much worry about hiring men. Quite often, the contractors, particularly those responsible for engraving and wood checkering, would hire men from Winchester, Ithaca, etc. to work on a temporary basis during their slack seasons. Of course, such an arrangement could not last as labor came into its ascendancy, and with the coming of unions and their restrictive contractual provisions it ceased entirely. As a result quality as well as production inevitably suffered.

The wage scale of gun mechanics and technicians is an interesting subject in itself. I have made an effort to ascertain at least some basic figures for this part of Parker history, but because so few of the old-time employees are still living, and since the contract system of hiring, just mentioned, makes definite wage scales for these employees variable, I have unfortunately met with very little success. The fact that Mrs. Hanson, the checker, was hired in 1908 at a starting salary of $.50 a day for ten hours work says much about the economic conditions of the time.

Mr. H. L. Carpenter, for many years office manager of Parker, recalls that about the turn of the century a first class gun mechanic received from $.25 to $.35 an hour, a good salary for that time. Mr. Charles Parker, the firm's last president, recalls the fact that in the late 1920's some of the department heads made $.90 an hour, certainly an excellent salary for this period. When one considers that this compares with the 4 to 5 dollars an hour gun makers get today, the comparison certainly tells a lot about economic change in the United States during the last half century. It also explains quite clearly why the good-quality double is now a thing of the past in the United States and why the only one still available, and that only on special order, costs $1200. It has been estimated that, under present production costs, it would require a retail price of $380 to make a double of the type which was sold by one company in the U.S. for $38.00 in 1938.

Length of service was naturally a distinguishing feature of Parker's employees. When the company was purchased by Remington in 1934, some of the older men in the plant had rolled up a very impressive record indeed. At that time, two men had been with Parker Brothers for more than fifty years. Two had served for over forty-five years; six, for over forty; three, for over thirty-five; two, for thirty; and at least five for twenty-five years.

The combined service records of these men made up a total of more than 720 years, a group average in excess of thirty-six years.

The history of the factory as an institution and the lives and careers of its employees are of course intangibles which facts and figures, interesting as they are, can never reveal in their true human significance. The work done by these men and women and its effect, however, are indelibly stamped on every Parker gun which ever left the factory.

CHAPTER 8

Production and Distribution Methods

Theory and Practice of Gun Building

THERE ARE, of course, different concepts in the building of shotguns as there are in the building of most mechanical products. A comparison of the concept followed by Parker with those employed by other gun builders proves very interesting.

In most of the European countries, such as England, Germany, Belgium, and Italy, the building of a high-grade gun proceeds in the following manner: a barrel maker will start a gun by making the barrels and will stay on this job until they are complete, from the forged or bulldozed tubes until the barrels are assembled with the lug, ribs, etc., are fully bored, and the lug machined. An action fitter will make the complete action, a stock fitter will fit the action into the stock and then shape and finish the stock, and so on for each part of the making and assembly of the gun. Each gun is an individual unit, with no parts being anywhere near interchangeable with the same parts of other guns. All parts are entirely hand fitted by a few individuals, each of whom does several jobs on the gun. This is one extreme in the theory of gun building and is the one followed by such famous firms as Purdey, Boss, Churchill, etc., in England.

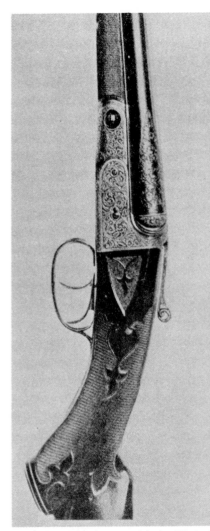

entire action was beautifully
keened; and from the tip of its
drawn muzzles to the toe of
shod, rubber-padded stock, ti
gun is truly,

"A thing of beauty, and a
ever:"—

A monument to its makers
lasting proof that not all of A
mechanical merit or artistic e
has been swamped in the mael
modern business competition.
deed gratifying to learn that the
means who wants and will pay
tistic effect in objects of utility
satisfied however exacting, and'
sending his money away from I

Individuality in Guns

Even the barrels of the
elaborately chased and engr
lanceolate effect. The sixteen
though different in its design, a
vidual—for no two of these
quality guns are, or in the n
things, can be alike; they are
of men subject to the limitati
dictations of the artistic tempera
is equally beautiful—but of th
later.

Handling, Pointing Proper

Needless to say, the gun im
perfectly as received, and was
given a through test to see if it
to its looks, the work being
later. Although its owner is n
shot, and never claimed better
per cent class at the elusive sau
managed to break about 70
with it at the first trial, and on
out into the field to try alignm
swinging powers on fast crossi
rocks, incomers, and all manno
verging angles, was forced to ad

An illustration in an article by Edwin L. Hedderly, published in *Western Field*, entitled The Small-Bore Shotgun, showing a top-grade small-bore Parker.

At the other extreme is the mass production concept used by many low-priced gun manufacturers. All parts are carefully machined to close tolerances, but are made so that the parts fit together with no hand filing or similar work but go together interchangeably with a tolerance between parts of, let us say, about .005 of an inch.

The system of gun making and assembly employed by Parker was a medium, which, between both these extremes, made use of the most desirable features of each while eliminating the unnecessary or undesirable aspects of both. The action parts were made up in large lots to close tolerances on the plus side. Barrel blanks in various sizes, cuts, lengths and bores were put up in the rough in batches. Guns then went through the shop in batches of twenty, which was generally a day's work for each man working on them. Each part had about .005 of an inch too much stock on it which had to be taken off by a file as the fitting together of the parts was accomplished. For example, when the lug on the barrel was fitted into the slot in the frame it would be pushed down into the slot with its sides covered with a paste made of oil and lamp black. Wherever it made contact as shown by the erasure of the lamp black, it would be carefully filed until it fitted all along both sides without quite touching. Thus, each gun was hand-fitted throughout just as in the case of fine foreign guns, but was made from uniformly machined components.

Weight and balance: the Parker factory always paid special attention to these two items. All Parker guns except those made with especially long or short barrels were made to balance at the point where the hinge pin

Wilber Fiske Parker shooting at the old Meriden Gun Club.

on which the barrels swing from the frame is located. In order to accomplish this by no means easy feat it was necessary to see that the proper weight was realized for the barrels and for the stock and action.

Let us say, for example, that the gun was to be a 20 gauge with 28 inch barrels to weigh six pounds. A certain weight stock had to be picked for this gun and no more or less than a certain amount could be "struck" or filed from the outside of the barrels. Parker Brothers always insisted that the balance was one of the most important elements in the successful shooting of a gun. A gun properly balanced will come up to your shoulder as if it were part of you; and if the length of the stock and the drops are right, a great deal has already been accomplished towards easing the job of the shooter. (Regarding the question of drop, more will be said and the point further clarified in the next chapter when the interesting Parker "Try Gun" is discussed in full). In commenting on drop, Mr. Charles S. Parker always expressed the personal belief that the most important stock dimension is the comb drop, because, if the shooter's cheek comes up to the stock in proper relation to the glance of sight down the top rib of the gun, then the heel drop, pitch, and stock length are not too important as long as the stock is not too long to make it difficult to bring the gun up to the shoulder.

At this point it is proper to mention that inspection, at any stage in the manufacturing process, played a very important part in the making of a Parker. A detailed description of this process shortly follows, but it should be noted that inspection was maintained at all stages from the selection of barrel and stock blanks through finishing and engraving. The head inspector was all-powerful, and his decisions could be overridden only by the plant manager, Mr. C. A. King, and later his son Walter King, or by Mr. Charles Parker, later Mr. Wilbur F. Parker, and later still Mr. Charles S. Parker. These men nearly always backed up the head inspector in his decisions, especially if the question was one that concerned the quality of the gun. This fact is worth mentioning because it played a paramount part in maintaining the quality of the gun. There might be many arguments, and there often were, between the various foremen and inspectors, but the inspectors never gave in without reviewing the case with the head inspector, who could at times become very unpopular around the shop.

All steel used in the gun was ordered by specifying tensile strength, transverse strength, plus strength to conform to a special test performed in the forge shop at the factory. The steel of a certain cross section and length had to bend back on itself when bent. Barrel steel was additionally tested by making sample gun tubes and blowing them up with overloads, and then testing the pressure they would withstand by the lead-plug compression test.

PRINCIPAL PARTS OF A DOUBLE GUN

Frame

In the total process of the making of a gun, we start with the action and its various parts, the most important of which is the frame. This is also the most complicated part, because from the time it is begun as a forging, until it is completely machined, 104 operations or cuts are taken on it. These include, among many others, milling, drilling, profiling, and nibbling.

Frames thus processed travel through this operation in batches of generally 100 at a time of one size and gauge. All the other component parts of the gun are likewise completely machined and ready for soft fitting and are carried in a stock room. All forgings are originally made on board drops in the forging department but in the later years of the company's existence they are to a large extent made by outside forge plants with Parker Brothers furnishing the steel.

Turning now from the frame to the other three principal parts of the gun, instead of following the order posited by the old metaphor of "lock, stock and barrel," an expression derived from gun making, we will consider these parts in the order of barrels, lock and stock, since this was the order in which the processing of the components was done at the factory.

Barrels

Perhaps the most important part of the gun is the barrels. From steel for stock, individual bars of proper length are set with one end up in a bulldozer. These embryonic tubes are then checked in a drilling lathe which spins them rapidly while a drill with one cutting edge puts a hole through them from one end to the other. This drill has a hollow shank cut with its one cutting edge so that oil under high pressure can be forced through the hollow shank of the drill and in this manner the oil used to carry the chips back out of the hole through the clearance space. Once in a great while a drill would run out through the side of a tube, bathing the ceiling, surrounding room and possibly the workmen with oil. This happened on one occasion when Mr. Walter King was taking a party through the shop.

The steel shavings and oil, forced out suddenly under such high pressure, created quite a furore.

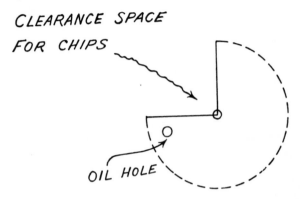

CLEARANCE SPACE FOR CHIPS

OIL HOLE

The tubes are then rough-turned on the outside on a lathe which has a form on the back of it to guide the cutting tool so that the tube tapers from one end to the other. Even at this point the tubes begin to become individuals. On each pair of barrels the tubes are turned to a certain form and thickness, so that where the tubes are assembled into the finished gun barrels the weight and shape must be just right for the gun of which they are to become a part. The tubes, which from this point on travel in pairs, are then machined at the butt end; and the forged and partially machined lug is brazed to the butt end of a pair of tubes.

This assembly, *i.e.* the two tubes brazed to a lug, is then heated and immersed in a hot tin solution so that all parts are completely covered with tin both inside and outside. The top and bottom ribs and the fore-end lug, all of which have been machined and tinned, are then tied into place by wiring them to the top and bottom of the tinned tubes. When this is done, square tapered nails are driven in under the wires to act as wedges.

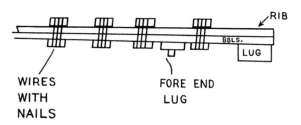

At this point it might be well to explain that in a double gun the center distance between the holes in the barrels is much greater at the butt end than at the muzzle. Consequently, it is necessary to bevel or curve the barrels so that they will shoot dead center at forty yards and will not cross fire. This particular task, one of the most difficult in the entire process of building the gun, is accomplished at this point by subjecting the barrels to the treatment known as "Englishing." This consists of hammering on the tapered nails which have been inserted under the wires and measuring the varying results of the relation of one barrel to another in the following way: The barrel assembler holds the barrels up and points them at a lighted glass which has a line across it. This line reflects down the inside of the barrel and the proper curvature of this line is obtained by the barrel assembler by loosening or tightening the wedges. Vast knowhow and experience are necessary in this job to get just the proper curvature of the barrels. The entire process demands the utmost skill, patience, precision judgment, and capacity for sustained effort. There is little wonder that expert barrel assemblers are few and in great demand at all times in the gun industry. The shortage of them in England, in particular, is one of the greatest handicaps in the gun industry there today.

After the trajectory of the barrels has been centered, they are next coated with pine resin and tin, allowing the fore-end lug and ribs to solder themselves to the tubes. Thus, the barrel properly curved comes into being. The barrels are then counterbored from the butt end to a point 6 inches from the muzzle by pulling through them rotating cutters called nut augers. This process is the beginning of the choke in the barrels.

The barrels are next bored and the choke cut into them. All barrels are full choke until the gun goes to final boring after it is practically completed. The Parker full choke is in the form of an ogive curve starting 6 inches from the muzzle and going to a point about ¾ of an inch from the muzzle, from which point on to the muzzle there is a straight section without curve or taper.

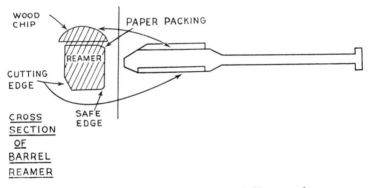

The reaming process proceeds as follows: the reamer is pushed through the barrel from the muzzle until it protrudes out of the butt. A long, wooden chip is placed on top of the reamer and the reamer starts to rotate; the barrels then travel horizontally, slowly pulling the reamer through the barrel, the reamer cutting as it goes. The cutting edge of the reamer is ground to the shape of the choke and is allowed to travel until it gets up into the muzzle end of the barrel where it gradually cuts or scrapes out the shape of the choke. After a cut has been taken, the reamer is backed out of the barrels and a long strip of paper is added under the wooden chip. This chip acts as a pressure plate and forces the reamer to cut more and more as each cut is taken, the workman adding additional paper packing under the chip as each cut is taken. After both tubes have been bored the barrels go to the stock room. Each pair of barrels has the weight stamped thereon.

The Locks

The making and assembly of the locks was a job involving the forging, shaping, filing and finally the fitting of a series of small, precision-built parts, each machined and then hand fitted to the finest and most accurate reciprocal functioning. Precision functioning is the ultimate and only goal of lock design and construction and in this part of the gun's structure Parker was as demanding as in all others. Building the locks was a complex process, involving as it did the fitting together of eighteen parts, until the amazing invention of Mr. James Hayes reduced that number of parts to four. In finishing the locks and the other parts of the mechanism, such as the ejectors, only the finest coil springs were used, and they were installed in such a way that, even should they break, they would still function so that the gun could be used. The locks used on Parkers were apparently always produced in the standard box-type of construction and housing. No mention of any other type of design has ever come to my notice, nor did the factory ever make up guns with detachable locks of the kind used, and even issued as a specialty. by Westley Richards in England.

The Stock

The same care and experienced judgment were used in the selection of the wood from which stocks for the Parker were made as were used for the purchase of steel and castings. Both domestic and imported wood were used by the factory, and the usual hand fitting was employed to insure perfect alignment between stock and frame. Selection of domestic wood received the personal attention of Mr. Walter King, who each year would travel to Des Moines, Iowa, where he would spend the better part of a week picking out the gun stock blanks, the majority of which he purchased from the Des Moines Saw Mills. These American Walnut gun stock blanks are crotch wood and were selected for figure in the stock and for as straight a grain as possible at the wrist or grip end of the stock. Although they had all been kiln dried, on arrival in Meriden they were carefully stacked in the loft over the engine room where a year's supply was held and allowed to air dry for twelve months before any were used.

On the more expensive guns, imported stocks of Circassin walnut were used which did not need this treatment. This wood went directly to the turning machines which roughed out the blanks and made the inletting cuts to take the tang of the frame and the tail of the trigger plate and trigger-guard bow. All stocks received this treatment, although a few blanks were left unmachined to be used on guns calling for very extreme or unusual stock dimensions. These stocks had to be entirely cut and fitted by hand.

THE BUILDING OF A PARKER GUN

Parker Brothers, in the overall plan for the building of their shotguns, naturally proceeded according to an approach which treated each gun as an individual project requiring a special and fully mapped out design. The engineering of a Parker was, in fact, a mechanical and artistic project comparable to that followed in the building of a fine automobile like a Buggati or Rolls Royce. When an order for a gun was received, a ticket was made out in the office showing the following information: grade of gun, gauge, barrel length, weight of gun, stock length, drop at comb, drop at heel, pitch of stock, type of butt plate, boring of barrels, ejector or non-ejector, single or double trigger, type of fore-end, finish of stock, and any other special features that the purchaser might desire. These tickets were white in color and accompanied the gun all the way through the building process from the selection of the first unfinished parts and blanks to the engravers.

Although Parker naturally received a large number of custom orders, the factory kept up a regular turnout of guns in the most popular models and built to the most popular specifications. These, and any guns not made to an individual order, were known as inventory guns and were placed on inventory listing in the stock room for shipment on inquiry or order for any type which happened to be made up. These shotguns were, of course, made in exactly the same way and with exactly the same quality of workmanship as any made to the most exacting and detailed individual order. The process was the same in both cases, the inventory guns being also accompanied from the beginning by a specification ticket which was blue in color. These tickets were first taken up by the men in the unfinished-parts stock room, who picked out a pair of barrels of proper length and weight for the gun.

For example, for a 20 gauge gun, with 28 inch barrels, the rough barrels should weigh 3 lbs. 2 ozs. and barrels with this figure stamped on their flats would be selected. The other component parts such as a frame of proper size (#0), the fore-end iron, trigger guard, trigger plate, a cut representing the parts that would join the barrels later on, were placed along with the rough barrels on one side of a balance-type scale. On the other side of the scale was placed a #6 cut. Then, stock blanks of proper grade and figure were selected according to the stock specifications on the ticket. The worker in charge of this process then placed a stock blank on the side of the scales with the barrels and other parts and proceeded to shift from one stock to the next until he had found one which exactly balanced the scales to the weight desired. On very rare occasions it was necessary to bore a hole in the butt end of the stock (to be later covered by the butt plate) to lighten it. Sometimes stocks were bored out and lead added to them when it was necessary to balance a heavy barrel and frame. This was another complicated and sometimes demanding process but one vital and absolutely necessary to achieve proper balance for the gun.

The barrels, stock and all the parts were then stamped with the gun number. In the case of very small parts, only the last three figures of the number were used. This is characteristic of the building of the finest product in a particular field. Reference has already been made to the similarity between the steps taken in the building of a Parker and those followed in the building of cars such as the Rolls Royce, whose makers quite justifiably claim for it the distinction of being "the best car in the world." It is significant that, in the building of a Rolls Royce, each and every part to be used is made with an extension on which is stamped the number of the particular car in which the part is to be used. These extensions are filed off each time a part is fitted. This process maintains the individuality of every Rolls Royce by giving individuality to even the smallest piece of the entire mechanism and thus marking every car as a distinct creation. This same individuality was stamped on every Parker shotgun turned out.

After the stamping of the parts, the gun moved out to the soft fitters where the frame was carefully fitted to the lug of the barrel. This was the most important fit of the entire gun and required precision workmanship of microscopic quality. The barrels had to close so that the standing breech of the frame fitted perfectly with the butt end of the barrels and the flats of the barrels and frame had to come close enough together to hold two pieces of tissue paper *but they must not touch each other*. All the other component parts were also soft fitted at this point. Another extremely precise and difficult fit was the trigger plate into the frame. In all Parker guns (except the Trojan Grade), and in Parker only, this trigger plate was shaped like a doll's head and the fit so carefully done that there would be no open spaces showing. In machining the trigger plate, this cut was milled in, a comparatively simple operation. On the frame, however, this cut was profiled in and the operator of the profiling machine had to be very careful to keep his cutter moving around the cut at a uniform speed because if he paused for a fraction of a second at any point the cutter would cut too much and when the trigger plate was fitted into the frame an open spot would result.

After being soft fitted, the gun parts were shoe-filed. The nose and sides of the frame were shaped up by hand filing as were also the triggers, trigger guard and balls of the frame. This operation called for men who were very skillful with a file and it was truly amazing to see what these workers could do with an ordinary file. After this the wooden gun stocks were fitted to their metal parts and were shaped up, proper drops established, and butt plates fitted. The stocks and fore-end woods were then removed and were finished with a coat of shellac and linseed oil. This finish was applied with a soft cloth, allowed to dry; then another coat was applied and the process repeated until the desired thickness and lustre finish was achieved. If an old English-type finish was specified, the wood was soaked in heavy linseed oil for about two weeks. Every day it was taken out, warmed up, and rubbed briskly by a hand cloth. Thus the linseed oil was soaked and rubbed in thoroughly and a superb finish resulted.

While the stocks and fore ends were being finished, the barrels were shaped and finished on the outside. This operation is known as barrel striking. All filing was done here lengthwise down the barrels by use of a tool which resembles a large cake of Ivory soap and is made with serrations, *i.e.* a file, on one edge. This is held in the hand and pushed up and down the barrel like a plane with the edge of the hand steering it down the barrel. This operation produced a long, smooth barrel with no waves in it. At the same time the top rib was struck and shaped. It had to be perfectly straight and true because the matting was then cut into it.

This was done on a machine which held the barrels firmly and then moved them slowly in a straight line under a cutting tool which oscillated back and forth cutting a single line at a time, after which the barrel was indexed a small amount and another line cut. And so forth.

Next for the barrels came the browning operation. It was this which gave them the true distinctive and famous finish which came to be a feature of Parker guns. This work took about two weeks and was accomplished by using the rusting process. The barrels were dipped in acid and then allowed to rust. They were then polished, dipped again, rusted and polished. This process was repeated twice a day for two weeks. The barrels were then cleaned and polished around the lugs and inside. Next the sight or sights were fitted, after which the gun was sent to the shooting room for final boring.

The actual process of targeting a gun will be separately considered at the close of this section of the present chapter. The Parker full choke and the method of obtaining it has already been described. The modified choke was accomplished by running the boring reamer up the barrel toward the muzzle so that practically all the straight section was eliminated. Improved cylinder and cylinder were obtained by running the reamer still further through the barrels thus eliminating practically all of the choke. When the barrels shot in a manner satisfactory to everyone concerned with the targeting of a gun, they were proof tested to insure absolute safety, and then stamped with the proof marks. Then they rejoined the rest of the gun for hard fitting.

Meanwhile the soft-fitted and shoe-filed parts of the gun were polished, engraved and given a bone-black case hardening before going to the hard fitters. During the case hardening operations it was not unusual for some of the parts to warp slightly. Although the soft fitting operation consisted almost entirely of filing, the hard fitting operation was one of bending, springing, and stretching the parts of the gun to the point that they once again fitted properly. This fitting operation was still another job which required an enormous amount of time, patience and personal skill. When it was finished the gun mechanism was assembled in its entirety and the sear ground to produce the proper weight for the trigger pull. It is interesting and significant, as an indication of Parker's attempt to leave nothing undone to produce the ultimate in a shotgun, to note that in fitting the screws into the gun all screw slots had to line up perfectly. If they did not, the screws were filed under the head until they fitted properly. This is a good example of the length to which the factory went to make the gun as nearly perfect as possible.

Now at last came the dreaded final inspection. The head inspector or Mr. King were the only ones who were authorized to exercise this function. If both of them happened to be absent, which was very infrequent, then Mr. Parker only had the authority to make this final inspection on which the reputation of the Parker Gun depended. Once a gun passed this inspection, the responsibility for any imperfection was on the shoulders of the head inspector and he was most careful indeed not to give Mr. King or Mr. Parker any reason to censure him. The head inspector had only 20 to 25 guns per day to inspect and few guns ever passed the first time they came into the inspection room. Nearly all were sent back for one or more minor touch-ups. Screws out of line, leaky barrel ribs, open places where metal parts fitted into the wood were examples of this. Very few guns were rejected for major defeats at this stage, for it must be remembered that the guns or their parts had been inspected all along the line after each new operation by other inspectors working under the guidance and authority of the head inspector.

As the gun progressed through the shop a record was kept in a large ledger in the final inspection room which indicated its progress all along the line until it arrived in the room for the head inspector's approval: this record was made from reports handed in by the inspectors each day. As the gun progressed through each of the various stages of being built, the successful completion of each one was recorded in the ledger. In addition to this record, all information on the gun was also recorded in a large book in the office in which was also later listed the name of the person or dealer to whom the gun was sold. These large books, now in the possession of the Remington Army Company in Ilion, New York, contain what is undoubtedly the largest, most comprehensive and most detailed record of the output of its guns, from order to delivery, maintained by any gun factory in the history of the United States. They are, in fact, a complete record from early in its history to the end of its life of the gun-making enterprise begun in 1865 by Charles Parker.

Targeting

I have chosen to describe the methods used to target a Parker shotgun under a separate heading, although this was of course a most important part of the total process of building the gun. I have made this decision not because the process itself is so lengthy that its mere size demands separate treatment. On the contrary, the

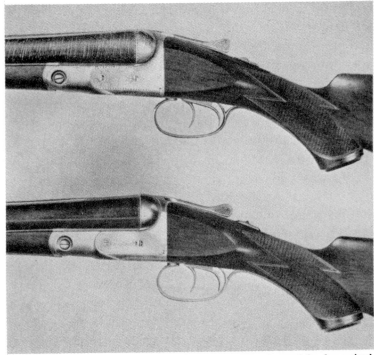

Quality P. H. and V. H. Grade guns to satisfy the demand for low-priced shotguns, "the best made of its grade ever produced."

description is very brief as the targeting method used by Parker was essentially simple. Its very simplicity, however, is apt to leave the impression that the process itself was not of great importance or that it was more or less a routine matter. Nothing could be farther from the truth. Targeting a gun (any good quality gun of any type) has always been an important and carefully controlled proceeding. After all, if a gun, though it be otherwise the finest product of the industry, does not shoot as it was built to shoot, it has failed to justify its sole purpose for existence. At the present time, the targeting of fine double guns and rifles in England is a process requiring such skill and experience that the gun industry is always behind on its orders from four months to a year for lack of qualified men in this and other fields.

For targeting at the Parker factory, the barrels were sent to the shooting room where a range and other devices were kept to test accuracy and patterns. In this room the barrels were locked in a fixed rest from which they were aimed at the center of a 30 inch steel plate standing forty yards away. This steel plate was mounted on a small car which traveled in either direction. The plate itself was painted white but had a bolt head in the center which was painted black. After each shot fired at it, the plate received a fresh coat of white paint, then was rolled back and the shots were counted by

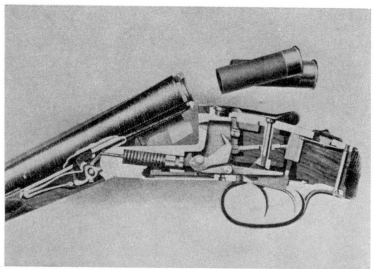

The above is from a single page advertisement relative to alteration, issued by Parker Brothers and carrying the New York Salesrooms address, 32 Warren Street.

painting them out with a paint brush. In this way the distribution of shot was noted and the percentage pattern was calculated.

In the so-called shooting room were two barrel boring lathes, and also a barrel straightening press. If the barrels did not shoot properly as to shot distribution and percentage of pattern, they were immediately rebored or straightened until they would fire dead center and produce the proper pattern. In this room also all barrels were proof tested for strength of the steel and single trigger guns were tested to make sure that they would not hook up or double. It was in this room that the final judgment was passed on the shooting qualities of the Parker Gun. It was thus a very important room in the Parker plant.

The entire process of building a Parker was, of course, a lengthy one. It is obvious from what has been said that such extreme care and attention to the smallest detail, much of it involving operations demanding absolutely flawless workmanship, could not be accomplished without a rather large amount of time. The actual amount of time required to build a Parker Gun varied with certain factors, such as the time of year (whether in the busy fall season or one where the number of orders was smaller), the amount of skilled labor available, and whether or not the purchaser had specified any details of design which necessitated greater care or extra labor.

But most of all it depended on the particular grade in which a gun was to be made. During the twenties and thirties, when production was at its highest, the period of time required to make a Parker of the highest, the medium and the economy grade was as follows: for the A-1 Special about six months, the engraving taking from six to eight weeks. All of these and usually the next highest grades were put through on special orders only from the start. For the D.H.E. about three to four months, so guns of this grade and those just below it were often semi-finished and held in rough stock for completion in accordance with a specific order. For the Trojan about eight weeks. This and the next several highest guns were often completed and put into inventory stock. This occurred as a result of the fact that, as the factory's lowest priced models, they were the largest sellers and so a certain amount of orders in the most popular specifications could be anticipated. Anyone who owns a Trojan, the cheapest gun Parker ever turned out, may well take pride and satisfaction in the fact that two months of hand-crafted work went into making it.

DISTRIBUTION AND SALES

The policies governing distribution and sales which Parker Brothers followed were entirely in keeping with both the conservative nature of the firm in general and its constant emphasis on individual skill, knowledge and long personal experience in the gun line. That is to say, they reflected the practice and outlook of a concern which had risen to occupy the place of honor in its field and thus did not have to rely on advertising to a great extent but which did believe that a man with a lot of personal technical knowledge was the best man to sell their product. These facts are first noticed when any student or collector of shotguns attempts to find old advertising material on the Parker. It is practically non-existent. This does not mean that it never existed but does indicate that advertising as a means of sales promotion was not of prime importance in the marketing of the Parker Gun.

Of course, the factory was small in comparison to many arms factories and so did not require large quantities of advertising to make its one firearm widely known. But the fact was that Parker apparently needed very little if any advertising to make its gun sell. The gun itself had done that from the beginning, and is still doing so to the greatest extent of any shotgun ever made in the United States. If, as far back as 1880, anyone had asked the question "What's in a name?" in reference to Parker, anyone who knew anything about guns would have instantly answered "Everything."

Any product which is first in its own line seldom requires advertising in volume to sell it; and the Parker, outside of the Company's own catalog, must have required little if any. As for the catalogs themselves, they, like the gun they featured, changed remarkably little through the years. This will become evident during a discussion of the Parker line itself as it was reflected in the Parker catalogs, and such a discussion follows in the next chapter. It is even more clearly apparent if the various grades are listed in tabular form. One of the appendices contains such a listing taken from all the catalogs which have come to hand, and these tables reveal at a glance that Parker was certainly the most conservative and at the same time the most successful producer and developer of shotguns this country has ever seen.

As for actual advertising in the usual public media, the company kept its usage to a minimum. The writer of this book has the advantage of living in Washington, where library facilities are unexcelled by those of any other city. The great Library of Congress, in particular, has an enormous collection of periodicals and newspapers. A fairly careful perusal of a number of the old sports magazines, particularly those devoted to hunting or the use of guns in any form, reveals a very small number of Parker advertisements and those which did turn up were conservative and almost modest in comparison with certain others. Wherever one does appear, the contents leave no doubt that the company was well aware of its prestige, aware enough to know that little more than the mention of its name and address were required to inform the reader of the nature and reputation of its product.

The present writer has also made efforts to locate window boards and other dealer's displays, but none have come to hand and those Parker employees with whom he has been in communication do not remember any such material ever being used by the company office. The probable explanation is that by the time this type of advertisement became widespread the gun's reputation was such that there was no need to make use of it. When Remington took control of the firm in 1934, the purchase was announced in all the sports magazines and many advertisements accompanied these announcements. These, like those of previous years, were dignified and circumspect, the main theme being that quality would prevail.

The firm's policy covering sales and distribution of its guns can also be well termed conservative. The first fact which requires mention here is that Parker, until its absorption by Remington, accepted individual orders for guns from almost any country in the world, something which most American gun makers discontinued after the first World War. The factory liked individual taste and felt very much at home in catering to it by individual communication with the prospective buyer. It also welcomed personal visits by anyone interested in the gun and its manufacture.

One of the most unusual Parkers I have ever examined is owned by a Washington real estate man. It is a 12 gauge long range gun, with a 36 inch barrel and a most unusual fore-arm grip in the shape of a beveled square block. The barrels are almost the longest I have ever examined on any type of shotgun and the fore arm, so far, is unique. He arranged for the design during a trip to Meriden in the late 1920's. There are, no doubt, other highly unusual Parkers in existence, as the factory made a specialty of making guns to the customer's most specific tastes so long as he did not request anything that would have compromised the gun's quality.

In the general distribution of their guns, the Parker Company preferred to make sales through either large and nationally-known concerns or through small but highly skilled gunsmiths or specialty shops. When Charles Parker first founded his Company in 1832, he sold his product first by cart and then by rail. Later, as markets expanded, he sold through large and well-known jobbers such as Belknap, Shapleigh, Weed and Co., Hibbard, Spencer, Bartlett, etc. This again reflects the keen business sense of the old Yankee industrialist. He knew that a product is best sold by one who already is experienced in selling, has a reputation, and a good clientele.

Parker Guns were handled as a specialty item by such firms as Stoeger and Abercrombie and Fitch in New

York, Edward K. Tryon in Philadelphia, Von Lengerke and Antoine in Chicago, Simmons Hardware in Kansas City, Phil Baekert in San Francisco, etc. This of course is to be expected, as the names of these firms signify in the gun business what the name Parker itself signified in the gun-making world—integrity, expert knowledge and careful advice and selection for the customer's need. In other areas, however, Parker preferred to sell its gun through small but expert gunsmiths or gun dealers, men who, if their business was not of great volume, were at least expert and reliable men in their field and who would have the knowledge of men who knew as a necessity of their trade the nature of a gun s design and mechanism and who could give sound and expert advice on the selection and fit of a gun.

In consideration of this policy it should be remembered again that the Parker was a custom-built product and built by more careful and individual skill and attention than was ever lavished on any other gun produced in this country. Finally, the skill and quality which a company can muster are of little use if a gun is not suited to the one who is going to use it. It was this desire for definite know-how in the advising and fitting of a gun for a customer which was back of Parker's desire to have its guns sold only by men who were perfectionists in the art of selling and selection just as it was Parker's never changing policy to have its guns made only by men who were the most skilled and talented in the trade, even to the smallest and most insignificant part of the process.

And this policy, like all Parker policies, paid off. It is indeed a rarity to find anyone even today, who complains of a Parker not being suited to his needs; and when this does happen it is nearly always the fault of his buying a gun, which, if its quality is beyond question, is not suitable for the shooter's build. Even this seldom occurs and when it does the owner has usually either been high pressured into buying the gun by a salesman or has bought it largely as a prestige piece without very much if any thought as to its suitability for his own use.

The divorce of the gunsmith from the actual business of selling guns for the last forty and more years, has been a very unfortunate aspect of the gun market in this country. When the sale of guns, like the sale of so many other products, has become commercialized to the point where a great deal of integrity disappears, the results for the consumer are bound to be unfortunate. Parker's policy was here as sound as it had ever been in any other aspect of the business.

Parker guns, although largely sold in the U.S. and Canada, were not by any means unknown in foreign countries. Tsar Nicholas' order for one is proof of that. More Parkers were sold in France than in any other foreign country and the name is still well known by French sportsmen of the older generation. The Parker company preferred Signet oil for use on its guns and recommended it by packing a one-ounce can with each gun. These small cans of Signet oil were sent to Parker by the Signet Company as advertising samples to be distributed free with Parkers.

As a finishing note on the care which the factory took to see that the preparation of their guns for the buyers was as perfect as possible, all shotguns were so packed that no movement of any kind was possible in transit. In addition, no part of any gun touched another part. To achieve this, some wood was used in all packing, but for the higher grade guns the boxes used for shipping were completely insulated with a light-weight but sturdy wood frame.

A very good example of the type of dealer who sold Parkers as a specialty is a shop which once existed in Washington but has now been out of business for some thirty-five years. It was located on Pennsylvania Avenue, South East, just to the right of the Library of Congress, near the beginning of that part of the avenue which runs in a straight line down an old, tree-lined grass right of way to the terminal overlooking the Anacostia River. The street and its shops were set up in the 1880's, as an extension of Pennsylvania Avenue, North West, on which are located the White House and other important government office buildings. This particular business was a combination of gun shop and gunsmith and owned by a man who knew guns as few in the business know them today. He had the Parker distribution for Washington for some forty years and prided himself on keeping the best stock of them in the area. High government officials, wealthy business men, Congressmen and Senators, diplomats and men who knew fine guns frequented his store.

One of his best customers was Judge Daniel Thew Wright of the old Supreme Court of the District of Columbia. Judge Wright, a gun lover and colorful Washington figure of a generation or more ago, was an admirer and collector of Parkers. He was also apparently an admirer of the Colt Single Action Frontier Revolver, for he carried one quite often which, on one occasion, accidently dropped from his pocket onto the floor of the beautiful man's room of the exclusive Cosmos Club, discharging, and alarming the guests while taking quite a sizeable chunk out of the figured plaster ceiling.

Judge Wright was an enthusiastic hunter and shooter and managed to collect a total of eighteen Parkers of all grades, gauges and styles. This, to the writer's knowledge, is the largest single accumulation of Parker guns ever made by one man. Unfortunately, the collection was disposed of by the judge's heirs following his death, and the present location of the guns unknown.

Outside of the factory stockroom in Meriden, the only salesrooms which Parker maintained were in New York City. There was apparently a sufficient demand for the gun in the New York area to make a company-owned store feasible, since the Parker catalogs list one for a period of nearly sixty years. From catalogs which I have been able to examine, the store apparently was opened

Meriden Gun Club. A. C. du Bray in center of picture and Wilber Parker in middle of firing line.

about 1870 or shortly thereafter and remained in operation until at least 1930. It is mentioned, possibly for the last time, in the catalog for that year and no mention of any New York salesroom is made in the Parker catalog for January 1, 1934, issued six months before Remington took over control of the firm, and the last catalog to be issued by Parker as an independent concern. The earliest description of the Parker line of shotguns which has come to hand, one which no doubt gives a very accurate indication of what the factory had done in its earliest years of gunmaking, is an advertisement on the last page of *The American Sportsman* for April 4, 1874. This lists the factory's "New York House" address as 83 and 85 Duane Street. How long it remained in this location is unknown; but by just before the turn of the century, and possibly at some time before, it had moved to 96 Chambers Street, a block which today houses some important gun and sporting goods firms, and was described in the 1899 catalog as the New York Showrooms. Sometime after the turn of the century the store again moved, this time to 32 Warren Street, in the heart of the city's sporting-goods area, where it remained until about 1916, as indicated by the fact that this is the address listed in the catalog for that year. The 1917 catalog gives it as 25 Murray Street, indicating that the next move had been made in either that year or the preceding one.

The catalog for January 1, 1930 still gives the Murray Street address, but this catalog was issued only about four months after the disastrous stock market crash of October 29, 1929. Since no New York salesroom is listed in the 1934 catalog, the New York facility probably closed within a year after the economic explosion which

Arthur C. du Bray, a Parker salesman and San Francisco representative.

heralded the depression and which was, within three years, to force Parker Brothers to sell the entire gun business to the Remington Arms Company.

To the writer's knowledge, the New York salesrooms which Parker maintained for so many years were the only such facility kept by any American gun maker in the New York area or for that matter anywhere else. By the 1920's most gun makers had even discontinued all mail sales and were selling only through dealers. The only other direct-retail-sales store kept by an American arms firm during this time was, to the best of the writer's knowledge, that operated by Ivor Johnson in Boston which, in addition to that firm's line of guns, carried guns of many other makers and perhaps the largest line of sporting goods in Boston. The salesrooms in New York City where Parker guns were sold as a direct factory outlet thus add another unique episode to the company's history. They also form another part of Parker's effort to provide, wherever possible, the personal touch of the expert, here the factory's own experts, in the sale of their guns.

Another and quite interesting type of salesmanship used by Parker was the display of its guns and their shooting qualities by men who were themselves expert shots and thus highly qualified to demonstrate on the spot what a gun is capable of doing. This is yet another form of gun display and merchandizing which has faded away with the passing of years. For many years before and after the turn of the century all of the major American gun makers employed professional exhibition shooters, some of them the finest in the world, to publicly display and sell their guns. Two outstanding examples of this are the world famous Buffalo Bill Cody, whose demonstration of the .44 Smith and Wesson to the Grand Duke Alexis resulted in that excellent revolver being adopted by Russia and being named the ".44 Russian," and Ad Topperwein, who, with his wife Plinky, was famous all over the nation for many years for his astounding shooting with Winchester rifles.

Parker was certainly not unaware of the possibilities of this sales technique and in fact maintained for many years a traveling force of shooting salesmen. These men went all over the continent, from the forests of Canada to the plains of Mexico, demonstrating the Parker. A good example is Mr. Arthur C. du Bray whose picture is reproduced here. Mr. du Bray was the West Coast exhibitor and sales representative for Parker with offices in San Francisco. His name was often listed by means of mailing card advertisements for Parkers. Here, again, was the personal touch of the expert, not merely the expert in knowledge of guns but in shooting them and giving a palpable demonstration of what a Parker would do. How much some of us today would like to see and enjoy this old-fashioned skill and the charm of the expert when deciding on a gun.

CHAPTER 9

The Parker Line

PARKER BROTHERS maintained consistently for nearly fifty years what was, to the present writer's knowledge, the largest line of double-barrel shotguns ever put into production, much less maintained, by any American gun maker. This is a fact which is indeed worth noting on its own merits, but when one reflects that the entire line was of premier quality and produced as the nearest thing to perfection at the time it is little short of phenomenal. Of course, the fact that Parker produced only one type of gun and had devoted itself from the beginning to the finest product possible goes a long way to explain this unique circumstance. But whatever the explanation, the very fact that the company maintained such a consistently large and stable line of guns is in itself an indication of the Parker's reputation and quality.

A glance at the Parker catalog for almost any one year in comparison with the catalogs of other makers of the same year demonstrates this fact. Let us, for example, compare the guns listed in the catalogs of the five principal American makers of doubles for that last year of fairly stable world peace, 1938. A numerical breakdown of the various makes by total number of different models produced reveals the following figures:

Parker	11
Fox	9
Ithaca	9
L. C. Smith	9
Winchester	6 (all of the same model)

A similar comparison, made by checking an old catalog from one of New York's largest stores, provides about the same ratio. The Von Lengerke and Detmold catalog for 1922-23 shows the following figures:

Parker	9
Fox	4
L. C. Smith	4
Ithaca	4

The A. F. Stoeger catalog for 1933-34 shows the number of models offered for the leading makes as follows:

Parker	9
Fox	7
L. C. Smith	9
Ithaca	8
Winchester	4 (all of the same model)

A comparison of the models listed in the Parker catalog for 1934 with those listed in the Fox catalog for the same year shows Parker offering a total of nine double guns and Fox a total of eight.

The Parker Pocket Catalog of 1917 offers a total of ten doubles, while the same type of catalog issued by Fox for the same year lists six.

In considering the actual line of guns manufactured by Parker, the first and most obvious observation to be made, and one, incidentally, which has already been made, is that from the beginning the firm manufactured but one type of gun—the double-barrel shotgun. The only exception to this was the single-barrel trap gun, and this, not added to the line until quite late in the firm's history, is, from the mechanical standpoint, really a variation on the double gun, since essentially the same mechanical problems and operations are involved in the manufacture of both types.

From time to time the factory technicians and engineers made experimental pump guns and automatics but never seriously considered adding them to the company's output. This decision was caused by the fact that such guns are made with rather loose fits and the factory was, for this reason, never able to design one commensurate with Parker quality. This, of course, settled the question of trying to market a repeater.

They also experimented with over-and-under guns but here, too, it was not possible to turn out one which was mechanically satisfactory in relation to Parker standards. The principal difficulty in this case was created by the fact that, in an over-and-under double, off-set firing pins are necessary unless one hammer is swung down from the bottom of the frame and the other from the top. This caused mechanical complications which the company did not like. In addition, the ejector mechanism was found to be too light and flimsy. For these reasons an over-and-under double, though the type was very popular after the first World War, was never marketed.

The factory, from the beginning, kept a large and carefully chosen stock of fine fittings for its guns, although it never actually made such accessories. Some of these fittings are listed and shown in the 1937 Parker catalog. They seem to indicate that Parker preferred the English-type trunk case for its guns followed by the French leg-of-mutton design. Here also the emphasis is on quality and lasting value, for any sportsman who has ever owned gun cases of this design or compared the various types knows quite well that there is nothing as sturdy, reliable and long lasting as these two. It is indeed to be regretted that the English trunk case seems now to be a thing of the past. At least none are listed in American catalogs and they are apparently available only in Europe, if there. Cases supplied by Parker during its lifetime certainly lived up to the old adage "a good gun deserves a good case." The factory supplied only the best, when asked to supply any at all.

It should also be mentioned that Parker Brothers never, at any time in the company's history, manufactured shells or ammunition components of any kind. The question is not likely to arise in connection with the company's later years, although it is brought up from time to time when occasioned by the finding of an old brass shotgun shell with the company's name on it. These are very desirable collector's items for anyone interested in ammunition and make quite a specialty in themselves. Of course, this type of shell became obsolete many years ago and was a product of the age when many gun owners wished to save money and bother by re-loading their own shells many times.

During the years after the Civil War, particularly in the 1870's and 1880's, such shells were widely sold, especially in rural regions where they were often a real convenience and practical aid and were offered by all makers of shotgun shells in the United States. In this connection it is interesting to note that even as long ago as the advent of single-case ammunition, there were never as many individual makers in the United States as there were in other countries. From the beginning, ammunition making in the United States has been concentrated in a small number of concerns which never at any one time have numbered more than six or seven. It is true that there have, from time to time, been smaller makers who concentrated on shotgun shells and .22 rim fire ammunition, good examples being Star, Robin Hood and American Eagle. These, however, were in business for only a few years and their products were never widely sold. They do, however, form a contrast with the present when sporting ammunition in the United States on any scale, is manufactured by but four firms, two of which specialize in only one or two types.

This is still not the rule in quite a number of other countries, particularly in regard to shotgun shells. In Spain, for instance, quite a few individual gunsmiths load their own shells to a customer's individual specifications and in England at least six of that nation's top makers of double guns offer proprietary shells, viz: Purdey, Boss, Greener, Powell, Gibbs, Grant and Lang. This is a holdover from the turn of the century when nearly every gun maker in Great Britain and the majority on the continent offered his own ammunition, particularly shotgun shells.

These facts, interesting in themselves, are important here as they form a background and contrast for the shells offered by Parker before 1900. These shells, as mentioned previously, were all of the old fashioned brass or nickel type and were all made for Parker by contract. The writer has been unable to discover who the maker was but it could very easily have been the old Union Metallic Cartridge Company or perhaps Winchester. Both made brass shells in quantity; but so far as can be determined, Parker never offered any paper shells under its own name. The metallic shotgun shells were stamped PARKER BRO'S, WEST MERIDEN, CT. and were available in 10, 12, 16 and 20 gauge.

It is worthy of note that, though Parker shotgun shells were not made by the firm itself, their very existence seems to add another quite possibly unique aspect to Parker history, as they were, to the present writer's knowledge, the only shotgun shells ever sold under such circumstances in the United States. The writer of this book is a collector of shotgun shells, and has, for some years, sought many unusual examples, particularly those made in the United States and Canada. During this time, neither personal search nor contact with outstanding collectors has ever, with the sole exception of Parker, turned up any shotgun shell, brass or paper, stamped with the name of any American maker of a shotgun. (It is to be understood, of course, that this does not apply to Remington and Winchester both of which have customarily carried good quality doubles in their line but never specialized in them. The comparison of Parker with other American shotguns implies, usually, those specializing in good or high quality doubles—Fox, Ithaca, L. C. Smith and Baker.)

Just why Parker Brothers put out a brass shell under its own name is an open question. It would not seem strange except for the fact that no other gun maker other than the big firms which made ammunition as a standard part of their line, ever did so. Almost no information about these old Parker shells has come to light during research on the gun itself. Mr. H. L. Carpenter, now 82 year old, who began work at the Parker plant in 1892, has no definite memory of shells ever being sold or offered by the company and never, during the 45 years he was on the job, saw any boxes of shells labeled Parker. This seems to indicate that these shells were offered during the 1870's and 1880's, when they were most popular and when Parker was expanding its line and establishing its reputation.

The most probable explanation back of them is that Charles Parker, already selling quite a line of miscellaneous hardware, and anxious for the success of his shotgun, decided to try brass shells under his name at a time when they were selling well. We can be fairly sure that those with his name did sell very well and that he only cancelled the contract for them when the paper shells started selling to the extent that they replaced the brass type. Whatever the circumstances, the old brass and nickel shotgun shells, sold by the makers of Parker Guns, add another unique feature to the history of the premier shotgun with so many other "firsts" and "onlies" to its credit.

When we come to examine the line of shotguns made and sold by Parker Brothers as an independent firm for some sixty-five years, two striking facts are immediately apparent: first, (and previously mentioned), that the total number of different models offered at any one time is surprisingly large, even though the company built only one type of gun; second, and much more significant, that the line itself remained almost constant over a period of many years, showing, in fact, only some half-dozen additions and withdrawals during a span of about forty years.

As far as actual factory production methods were concerned, the manufacture of such a line required the maintenance of a very diversified inventory of frames. Parker guns were made up with different size frames and parts depending on the gauge and weight of the gun. These frames and sizes of guns were classified by numbers as follows:

> #3 —8 and heavy 10 gauge
> #2 —light 10 gauge and heavy 12
> #1½—light 12 gauge and heavy 16
> #1 —light 16 gauge
> #0 —20 gauge
> #00 —28 gauge

Such a large variety of sizes inevitably meant a large inventory of machined parts, but careful discrimination of parts and frames, as the first steps in production, made for a much better handling and balanced gun.

For factory convenience in inventory and other records, the various grades of guns also went by numbers. The following list gives the number used for each grade and the percentage of a normal year's production occupied by each grade:

> Trojan—Trojan—40%
> Vulcan   #0 —25%
> PHE   #1 — 3%
> GHE   #2 —10%
> DHE   #3 —15%
> CHE   #4 — 1%
> BHE   #5 — 5%
> AHE   —#7 ⎫
> A1 Special #8 ⎬ 6 to 8 per year
>   ⎭

In normal years, about 4,000 guns were made, although this figure varied considerably from one year to another or between certain years. The distribution of grades produced, as shown above, was fairly constant, especially in the higher grades where the number made was small in any year. The Trojan, or economy model,

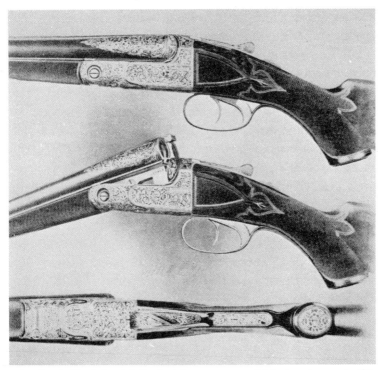

Quality A. No. 1 Special, "embodying every essential feature known to the most skillful craftsmen in the gun-makers art."

was always the big seller from the time of its introduction followed by the Vulcan or VH. Next to these, the largest seller was the DHE, which in the early 1900's was known as Parker's $100 grade gun.

1874 Advertisements

Although no factory literature covering the very early Parker line has come to light during the research on this book, one particular item has been discovered, which is fortunately quite sufficient to reveal a substantial amount of information about the early manufacture of

Parker guns. This is a volume of an interesting, old sports magazine, *The American Sportsman*. Devoted entirely to hunting, fishing and natural history, it was published by Wilbur F. Parker, son of Charles Parker, who had offices in West Meriden, Connecticut and New York City. With the format of a small newspaper, it was published every Saturday. The volume which has turned up covers the period April to October, 1874 and is numbered Volume IV.

A persual of its pages very quickly reveals that Wilbur F. Parker, the editor and proprietor, was most anxious to have the opinions and contributions of all types of leading authorities in the fields to which his magazine was devoted. The pages are filled with letters, articles, editorials, etc. by many experts on shooting, ballistics, dogs, plant and animal life, and nearly everything related to the use of a rod and gun in the outdoors. Many of his contributors were top scientific authorities and administrative officials, such as those employed by government agencies like the Smithsonian Institute, Department of Agriculture and Department of the Interior.

This rare work was part of the library of the Friendly Club and Institute of Meriden, Connecticut, where it was often used by the Meriden Gun Club members. It apparently went back into the possession of the Parker Company, from where, along with a great many Parker records and papers, it was taken to Ilion, New York, when Remington took over. There it became part of the plant library of the Remington Arms Company.

Like all magazines, *The American Sportsman* accepted advertisements for merchandise related to its own subject matter and the last two or three pages of each issue are filled with many interesting offers of hunting, shooting and fishing supplies commonly used in the 1870's. The most common of these is certainly the double-barrel sporting gun, for which advertisements from many makers and dealers are listed. All are very interesting as they reveal the wide scope and variety which the double gun enjoyed in its earliest years of modern design.

A rather intriguing one which reveals something of the practices prevalent in the competitive side of the gun business of that period is a warning from the famous English gun maker, W. W. Greener of Birmingham. Addressed to American sportsmen, it cautions them strictly to beware of "the vile German imitations" of Greener Guns which are "descending on the States in a flood" and are "utterly undependable." Apparently, the practice of German firms dealing in low-class double guns was as much of an annoyance and threat to the makers of the good ones as the cheap Spanish imitations of Colt and Smith and Wesson revolvers were to those firms in the 1920's and 30's.

It is interesting to note in this connection, that although no Parker literature which I have ever examined makes any mention of counterfeit or imitation Parkers, a gun catalog put out by a large Pittsburgh dealer, of the 1890's, J. H. Johnston, warns his customers that fake Parker guns are often sold by gun stores for twenty to thirty-five dollars and that all genuine Parker guns bear the stamp "Parker Bros., Meriden, Conn." Mr. Johnston places this observation under his listing of the Parker Hammer Gun and so does not make it clear whether the warning applies equally to the hammerless models. In any case. whatever attempts were made to pass off counterfeit Parkers to the public, the factory apparently never regarded it as a serious threat or one even requiring mention in its own catalogs.

Wilbur Parker was, to be sure, quite willing to accept advertising from many makers and put it on the same page of his own magazine with the offers of his own gun. It is true that the Parker ads were usually the largest and it is from them that we discover the format of the Parker line in 1874.

An examination of the advertisements for Parkers in *The American Sportsman* for April 4 and May 30, 1874 reveals instantly one outstanding fact, a fact which was to characterize the Parker line for the entire remaining span of its life, a period of some seventy-three years: within six years after the first Parker had been placed on the market the gun had met with such success that the factory could proclaim it to be "The best and hardest shooting gun in the world" and offer it in the amazing total of eleven different models, ranging in price from forty-five to two hundred and fifty dollars. It is probable that this same line of guns was available several years earlier, but whatever the exact year in which this number of guns was first offered, the fact that, by six years after its emergence into the gun market, the Parker was available on an ascending scale of graduated quality on a plane comparable to exactly the same scale of values which it would maintain to the end of its life, is indeed a striking tribute to the industrial and technical ability, even genius, of Charles Parker and his staff.

Unfortunately, these advertisements for the spring of 1874 do not give any details of the guns themselves. Four facts are, however, apparent from the wording: the extensive scale of quality, indicated by the price range;

the general design of the gun is still the same as that of the first Parker, indicated by the picture of the gun's center section; the availability of a "variety of models," as expressed in the wording of the advertisments; and the very significant fact that within the short space of six years the Parker had proven itself in actual competetive shooting to the extent that it had chalked up the very impressive total of thirteen prizes, diplomas and various awards, as listed in the advertisement for August 1, 1874.

Two of these awards, which may be noted in the advertisement as here reproduced, are of outstanding significance. Previous to the date on which the magazine appeared, every first prize for trap shooting at the last convention of the New York State Association had been won with a Parker; in the year 1869, the *first* year following that in which the Parker had been placed on the market, it won a medal and diploma from the American Institute, an organization which judged manufactured products from every country in the world. So it was that within a year after being created, the Parker had established one of the many marks of honor which would distinguish it to the end of its long life, perhaps in this case the most honorable of all—the quality and character of proving itself as outstanding at all times among other double guns.

The actual mechanical nature of the Parker of 1874 is not precisely clear from what is known of the gun's history. That it featured the original Parker lifter mechanism, activated by a lever in front of the trigger guard, is obvious, as previously noted. But in this connection it is necessary to remember that it was in this same year of 1874 that Mr. C. A. King, known in future years as the father of the Parker, came to the Company from Smith and Wesson, and that his first contribution to Parker design was to improve the lifter mechanism. So perhaps the guns offered by the spring and summer of that fortunate year in Parker history had received the benefits of his talents. In any case, before 1874 Parker had, in five short years, emphatically and unmistakably become what it was to always remain: America's finest shotgun.

The 1874 advertisements' use of the phrase "various styles" suggests that the Parkers then available were built in many types as well as many grades. This is probably true, especially in view of the fact that the factory, from the beginning, always sought to offer a truly custom-built gun which could be produced to meet the customer's individual wishes. When it is also remembered that there was a larger variety of bore sizes available by the 1870's than was to be the case in future years, it seems a logical conclusion that many different types of Parker Guns were made in the company's first years, though probably in small number. The majority of early Parkers were certainly made with the straight stock. All pictures show them as having it and it was certainly the commonly accepted design for double-gun stocks until about 1880. Quite a number of early Parkers were no doubt made in .14 gauge, a popular size at the time and the one for which the first Parker shotgun was chambered.

One mechanical feature which had been an early addition to the Parker mechanism, and which is specially mentioned in the 1874 advertisements, is that of rebounding locks for which there is no extra charge. From this we may deduce that this particular feature was something new in double design at this time and that Parker, though it apparently had no patent on the device, was offering it at no extra charge. Certainly in the case of a Parker or any other double gun of this period, a device which prevented the hammers from impinging on the exposed firing pins after a shot had been fired would have been a most desirable safety feature.

From the statements of one of their advertisements, Parker had found it possible to reduce its prices and to call its gun the "cheapest" as well as the "best." From this I think one may safely conclude that the company was using a phrase which obviously meant cheapest of the higher-priced grade of doubles, or perhaps the cheapest price at which Parkers had been available to that particular time.

The early Parker advertisements invite the reader to write for a factory circular describing all models. If one of these previous early circulars had come to light during the research on this book, perhaps we would have more information on the earliest Parkers. That is, at least, certainly a future hope and possibility.

The fourth of these advertisements for mid-1874 displays an interesting shooting accessory marketed by Parker at that period, one which, to the present writer's knowledge, is the only item related to shooting other than the shotgun itself and the brass shells ever to bear the Parker name. It is a shell belt of very ingenious design called by the term "Clip Cartridge Belt." Bearing the patent of the Parker Company, it is made with suspender-type holders and is distinguished by the fact that it carries any size of shell equally well, and the special feature which holds the shell open end up, thus preventing the wads in loaded shells dropping out or becoming loose. Apparently this was a cause of complaint by many sportsmen of this period and no doubt resulted from the fact that many shells were then handloaded, resulting in improperly packed wadding which often came loose or even dropped out at the most inconvenient moment. Even in a small and rather common-type of shooting accessory, the Parker name thus meant something of unusual design and creativeness plus extra quality and skill.

1899 Catalog

The Parker Catalog for 1899 is an important one for several reasons and through it may be traced the gun's history across the decades of the 1880's and 90's. In addition, it presents the Parker shotgun on the threshold of the twentieth century, a time of important transition when the mechanical structure was about to leave its oldest feature behind and forge ahead with the most radical change it had adopted so far, a change which had by that time been proven by some eight years of usage. This very significant and rare Parker catalog is available because of the fortunate fact that it was reprinted in the interesting book *Ten Rare Gun Catalogs,* compiled by the well-known Chicago gun authority and editor, John T. Amber. Mr. Amber's collection of old catalogs covers the years 1860-1899, the Parker representing the latter date.[1]

This particular catalog has several features which make it unusual in itself. Although very detailed in its description of the Parker line, unlike every other Parker catalog I have examined, it has almost no illustrations of

---

[1] Originally published by Greenberg: Publisher: New York, 1952. Now the property of Chilton Publications, Philadelphia. Extracts reproduced here by permission of Chilton Publications.

the gun itself. The only two gun illustrations it contains are, in fact, center cuts of the hammer and hammerless models, meant of course to be representative of both types. It contains a very interesting special feature, a complete and detailed description of the manufacture of Damascus and twist steel barrels. There are also some notes on making extra barrels for guns of a different gauge.

The list of hammer guns in 1899 is, as the list here reproduced makes obvious, a very extensive one. A total of fourteen models is offered, five more than the hammerless type. The usual extra features, such as extra weight, extra-long barrels, and extra sets of barrels may be had for an addition to the price of the particular model. This very large line of hammer double guns, representing the usual Parker scale of quality and workmanship, is not a surprising fact in relation to the year in question. In 1899 the hammerless mechanism was still rather new in what was then technically considered, yet a conservative society. It had only been put on the market in the early 1880's and had not become a part of the Parker mechanism until 1889.

The first Parker guns with hammerless locks came on the market generally about 1890 or 1891. It is then not at all surprising that the old-favorite double gun should, only eight years later, still dominate the factory's production. So popular did it remain that, as we shall shortly see, the mechanism itself was not finally discontinued until the time of World War I, fairly late in the company's history. The remarkable appeal which the old hammer-type of double-gun mechanism has held and still holds over the preference of hunters and shooters is well illustrated by the remark of the world-famous

African ivory hunter, John Taylor, who declared, that if he could have but one rifle to use for the rest of his life, he would be quite happy to take an old fashioned English black-powder express rifle with outside hammers.

But there is one aspect of the Parker hammer guns for 1899 that is, indeed, most remarkable. The old lifter bolt mechanism, that which was the distinctive feature of the first Parker gun ever produced, is still available for those who wish it. It cannot be determined how many guns were actually still being produced with this original Parker feature at this time. It may well be that it was not actually produced as a stock item at all but only kept in the catalog to attract the trade of old timers or those who had grown accustomed to the lifter action in their first experience with a shotgun. Even if this was the case, however, the simple fact that the factory could still feel financially justified in offering guns made with a mechanism fourteen years out-of-date (the top lever had been introduced in 1882), is a most impressive indication of the confidence which the American shooting public had in the original Parker design and the popularity which it still enjoyed.

By 1912, and quite possibly within several years after the turn of the century, the lifter action had been completely discontinued, but the more than thirty years of success which it had achieved constituted the particular factor which made the Parker the firm and lasting success that it had by then become.

An examination of the Parker hammerless gun available just on the threshold of the twentieth century reveals several interesting facts. The list offers a line of hammerless models which, with several exceptions, was very much the same as it was at the time of the first

World War and, for that matter, what it was largely to remain. The exceptions, however, are interesting and require a word of comment. First, the standard top-grade Parker is here given as the A.A.H. Pigeon Gun. The magnificent A.1 Special, which was to remain the standard top-grade Parker from the time it was introduced, had at this time not been put on the market. It was apparently first offered sometime between 1900 and 1912, since it is given first place in the catalog for the latter year. At the opposite end of the line, the very popular V. Grade Parker, of which more models were apparently made than any other gun in the line, is also not listed in the 1899 Catalog. Since it also appears in the 1912 Catalog, it can be assumed that the two Parkers which were, with the two exceptions which will be discussed later, the most expensive and least expensive guns in the entire line both came in at some time between about 1899 and 1912.

In addition to revealing the absence of the two guns which soon came to occupy the opposite ends of the scale, the 1899 Catalog reveals the presence of two particular grades of shotguns which are not subsequently listed and are, at least to the writer's knowledge, not mentioned in any other Parker literature. These are the E. and N. grades. The details for these two particular Parkers can be seen in the reproduction of the page listing hammerless guns in the 1899 catalog. Their existence at this time may, I think, be easily explained by the fact that the line had been expanding fairly rapidly, especially since the introduction of the hammerless mechanism, and that the factory desired to offer as large a line of models with this feature as of the corresponding hammer models. The hammer line for 1899

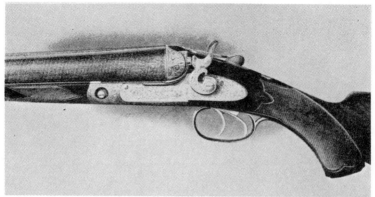

Nine models of hammer guns ranging in price from $400 to $55 were listed in January of 1912.

includes an E. grade though not an N. The additional fact that neither grade is included in either the hammer or hammerless line by 1912 is easily explained by the circumstances that by then the A.1 Special and V. grades had been added; and since the entire line had thus been extended to what was then the logical extremes, it was no doubt deemed best to drop two of the guns which were so close in quality and finish to those which followed and preceded them, that there was no real justification for their being continued. This same action was later taken with the P grade.

One page of the 1899 catalog is devoted to a description of the Parker Hammerless gun. The details stress, in particular, the spiral mainspring, the one-piece cocking slide which operates both hammers simultaneously, the long action frame and the patented rebound device, which insures absolutely that the hammer nose will not hang in the indented primer. Such modern and improved mechanical devices had been well calculated to insure the permanent success of the hammerless model, and coming as they did, during the decade of the gay nineties, had brought the Parker, on the eve of the new century, to the rank of first place in the field of double-barrel hammerless guns, a place it was to permanently occupy as its predecessor had that of first place among the earlier hammer models.

Continuing to survey the Parker line, we may now examine the 1912 catalog. This contains what had, by that time, become almost the full line carried by Parker when the firm ceased operations, a line containing the guns still remaining from the Nineteenth Century and carrying the more old-fashioned features, and with the exception of the economy-grade and modern-types of shotguns to be added in future years, the same models which every succeeding catalog to the very last issued was to display. Since most of these models had been in the company catalog since at least 1900, we are really getting another look at what Parker was producing at and before the turn of the century. It should be explained here that the designation of Parker models involves three classifications: quality; hammerless or hammer mechanism; and ejector or non-ejector type. Thus, VH = lowest quality, hammerless and no automatic ejector, V.H.E. = lowest quality, hammerless mechanism, with automatic ejector.

The 1912 Parker Catalog

V.H. and V.H.E. simple, border-line engraving around the receiver and base of barrels. 12, 16, 20 or 28 gauge. Vulcan steel barrels.

P.H. and P.H.E. Heavier line engraving, simple flourish designs. Barrels of English twist steel. 10, 12, 14, 16 or 20 gauge.

G.H. and G.H.E. More extensive flourishes, birds in

oval on sides of receiver. Barrels of either three-blade Damascus steel, nicely figured or Parker Special Steel without figure. 10, 12, 14, 16, 20 or 28 gauge.

D.H. and D.H.E. Scroll engraving, figure of bird dog in oval. Barrel of finely figured damascus steel or Titanic steel without figure Shield on stock. 10, 12, 16, 20, or 28 gauge.

C.H. and C.H.E. Heavier and more elaborate scroll engraving, figure of dog in oval on sides of receiver, figure of running deer on front of receiver. Engraved trigger guard. Barrels of finest Bernard steel, evenly figured; Damascus steel very finely figured; or Acme steel without figure. Silver Shield on stock. 10, 12, 16, 20 or 28 gauge.

B.H. or B.H.E. Still heavier and more elaborate scroll engraving, figure of dogs in oval on side of receiver, figures of running dog and deer on front receiver, engraved trigger guard and receiver extension. Checkered stock panels. Fore arm completely checkered. Barrels of extra fine Damascus steel, finely figured or of Acme steel without figure. Gold shield or name plate on stock. 10, 12, 16, 20 or 28 gauge.

A.H. or A.H.E. Heavier and more widespread engraving; dog in woodland scene on sides of receiver, not surrounded by oval; two scenes on front of receiver, smaller one showing dog at top, larger one showing dog standing over fallen deer at bottom. Checkered stock panel. Fore arm completely checkered. Gold shield on stock. Barrels of finest Damascus steel, finely figured or of Acme steel without figure. 10, 12, 16, 20 or 28 gauge.

A.A.H. and A.A.H.E. Lavish, rich engraving, completely covering receiver, receiver extension, and top lever and extending up the barrels about two inches.

All scroll, no scenes of any sort. Lavish checkering on stock, fore arm completely checkered; gold shield on stock; barrels of Whitworth fluid pressed steel. Certificate of the genuineness from the makers, Sir. W. G. Armstrong Whitworth and Co. accompanies each gun. (Also available in Damascus steel.) 12, 16, 20 or 28 gauge.

A No. 1 Special—with or without ejectors, as lavish engraving and checkering as possible to produce on a double gun, receiver and trigger guard completely covered, grip cap also checkered, engraving extends higher up barrel than on the A.A.H. Monogram gold shield or name plate, triggers heavily gold-plated. Barrel of Whitworth Steel, with certificate of genuineness. 12, 16, 20 or 28 gauge.

The Parker Hammer Gun

It is not, of course, to be thought at all unusual that the Parker catalog could feature, as late as 1912, a double-barrel hammer gun. On the contrary, the fact that the hammerless-type double had been in production for approximately forty years had not by any means diminished the demand for the older type to the extent that its production was unwarranted. The Parker hammer gun is still listed in the 1915 Catalog and was not removed until the end of World War I. In this connection it is worthy of note that the double hammer gun is still found in the catalogs of the larger mail order houses and sporting goods companies as late as 1934 and possibly later. Guns still sold at this late date were all products of makers who produced very low-priced guns, such as Davis Warner, Crescent, Eastern Arms, etc. They were the lowest priced guns possible to produce, but

Photographs, on this and the opposite page, were made by Leo J. Gallenstein of Washington showing Parker shotgun shells. In the illustrations showing 3 shells the one in center is nickel and 12 gauge; the other two are 10 gauge brass.

certainly reflect strikingly the fact that the double gun, even in its oldest design, was, as late as the early 1930's, one of the most popular weapons ever devised.

The Parker hammer gun, however, like all Parkers, was very much out of the category which could be called in any way ordinary. Like the Parker hammerless models, it was made in an ascending scale of quality from the lowest quality with simple engraving and checkering to the most lavishly-made gun possible to produce. The 1912 catalog lists a total of nine qualities, whose designation parallels to an extent the classification used for hammerless guns. The models are: T. R. H.

G. D. C. B. A. and A.A. Pigeon Gun. From quality T. through G. only Damascus or twist steel barrels were offered but from D. through A.A. modern-steel barrels were available, Acme or Titanic in D. through A.A., and Whitworth fluid pressed steel in the A.A.

Again, Parker is unique. The Parker hammer gun was the last American double-barrel hammer gun of top quality to be offered to the public; and by the time it was discontinued, it was the only double hammer gun built in the United States in such a variety of qualities. In fact, by the time Parker discontinued it, all the other American makers of good doubles had either discontinued hammer guns altogether or were making only one or two in a plain or economy grade. Here is another testimony to the esteem in which the Parker was held. The fact that it could offer what was, by 1912, an essentially obsolete design of gun in a full range of quality, and continue to offer it until the end of World War I, is an unmistakable indication not only of the popularity of the Parker but of the ability of the company to discern at all times what type of guns would be a sure success, if even to a limited extent.

The 1915 Parker Catalog

What if any new catalogs were issued between 1912 and 1915 is uncertain. The indications are, however, that none were issued and that in 1913 and 1914 the 1912 catalog was still used, possibly with flyers announcing new prices.

In any case, the Parker catalog for 1915 lists, with one very important exception, the same line of shotguns as the catalog for 1912. The grades for both hammer- and hammerless-types and the designs of engraving and checkering, are exactly the same as in the 1912 catalog. The only variation apparently was the fact that the P. quality gun was then offered with Parker Steel barrels, whereas in 1912 it was only available with Damascus barrels, an indication that by the time of World War I the old-fashioned steel barrels were already well on the way to replacement and only needed the war itself to bring this about. All miscellaneous information in both catalogs, such as that dealing with the design and construction of the gun and its mechanism, is also the same. The important exception referred to above is the Parker Trojan or Economy Grade Gun, listed first in the 1915 catalog. This model, which occupied nearly half of the factory's total production from its introduction until manufacture closed, will be discussed separately under special models at the end of this chapter.

The 1917 Parker Catalog

The 1915 catalog includes a flyer giving revised prices in effect as of January 24, 1916, obviously caused by the pressures of the war, which was to involve the United States in little more than a year. The next Parker catalog which has come to hand is that for 1917, a pocket catalog, which also includes a flyer listing revised prices in effect December 1, 1919. The war had not stopped production of Parker guns but had, as an effect, caused a price increase as indicated for the year 1917 itself.

The aftermath had brought still further increases, lifting the retail level once again by 1919. The factory had thus raised prices three times within the same number of years. The Parker pocket catalog for 1917, small in size, again lists with one exception exactly the same line of guns as the 1912 catalog. All models are available in hammer and hammerless types (except the V. and Trojan); all (except the P., V. and Trojan) are available with Damascus steel barrels; and all (except the Trojan) are available with automatic ejectors. This time the important exception is the addition of a single barrel trap gun, the only type of gun other than a double barrel which the Parker Company had offered since it started making shotguns in 1868. This model will also be discussed at the end of the chapter.

Parker during the Twenties

The wave of prosperity which visited the nation after the end of World War I brought increased production, modern improvements and innovations and some expansion to Parker as it did, in a greater or lesser measure, to all American gun makers. The nation had, after all, learned more about guns in the eighteen months of the first global conflict than it had learned in all of its previous national history, important though guns had been since the battle of Lexington and Concord. Of course, fine sporting guns of the type made by Parker are not usually directly affected by war except in the negative sense that production is often stopped in whole or in part. Even this did not occur to any noticeable extent. If Parker had any war production contracts during the period April 1917 to November 1918 no record of them has come to light and no mention of them has been made by anyone during the research on this book. If there were any, it seems safe to say they were on a limited scale. In any case, the factory continued making shotguns during the war and, during its last year, actually designed and produced the first exception to its line since the company had been making guns.

Quality A. A. H. E Pigeon Gun

With Automatic Ejector
Net Price $500.00

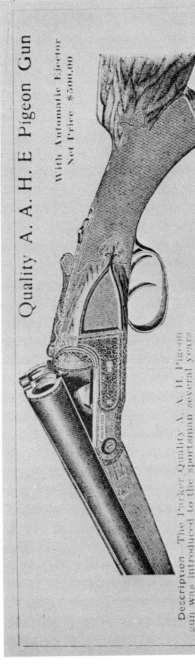

Description The Parker Quality A. A. H. Pigeon gun was introduced to the sportsman several years ago, and has proven a popular favorite to many who appreciate uniformity in performance and exactness in details together with fine workmanship, material and handsome finish.

Barrels The barrels are of Whitworth Fluid compressed steel accompanied by a certificate of genuineness from the makers, Sir W. G. Armstrong, Whitworth & Co., or the very finest Damascus steel. As a substitute for Whitworth barrels we furnish Parker Peerless Steel barrels, manufactured by us and carrying our unqualified written guarantee.

Stock The stock is of finest imported Circassian walnut, with gold shield; checkering and engraving only of the highest order and skillfully wrought; beautiful for its simplicity; skeleton butt plate.

Specifications Made in 12, 16, 20 or 28 gauge; straight, pistol or half pistol grip, or Monte Carlo stock; various weights, lengths, drops or measurements, or with special features. This is a handsome, durable and splendid gun.

A page from a catalog with price list dated Dec. 1, 1919.

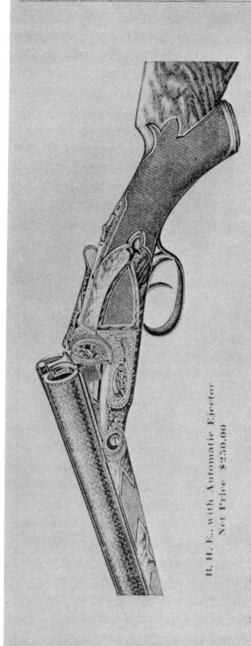

B. H. E., with Automatic Ejector
Net Price $250.00

Extra Fine Damascus or Acme Steel Barrels. Plate, Straight or Pistol Grip or Monte Carlo Extra Fine Imported Stock, Gold Shield, Extra Stock; No. 10, 12, 16, 20 or 28 Gauge. Fine Checkering and Engraving, Skeleton Butt

A page from the catalog dated Dec. 1, 1919, showing the B. H. E.

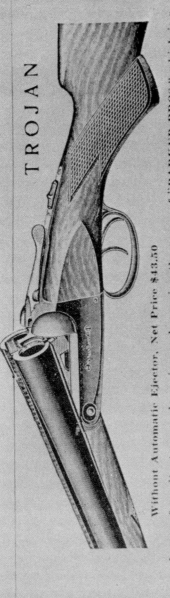

TROJAN

Without Automatic Ejector, Net Price $43.50

A Gun of merit, at a popular price, and carrying the name of "PARKER BROS." which is a guarantee of quality.

Barrels made of Trojan Steel, plain black finish. This steel is manufactured expressly for Parker Bros. Stock: American Black Walnut. Fore End and Stock neatly checkered. Cap Pistol Grip with plain finish. Hard Rubber Butt Plate. Drop about 2¾ inches. Length of stock, 14 inches.

Made to the following specifications only.

12 gauge 30 inch barrels, 7½ to 8 lbs. both barrels full choke.

12 gauge 28 inch barrels, 7½ to 8 lbs., right hand modified, left hand full choke.

16 gauge 28 inch barrels, 6½ to 7 lbs., right hand modified, left hand full choke.

20 gauge 28 inch barrels, 6¼ to 6¾ lbs., right hand modified, left hand full choke.

No deviation will be made from these dimensions, except they may be R. H. Cyl. and L. H. Mod. or Full Choke if desired.

The Trojan Model as illustrated in the December, 1919, catalog.

The impetus given to gun design and production in general, plus the widespread swing to modern improvements encouraged by the war, no doubt had an indirect effect on the company's policy. One effect which certainly resulted was, as already noted, the complete discontinuance of the supply of Damascus-type steel from Belgium and other European sources. This, in turn, resulted in the complete cancellation, within three years of the armistice, of the manufacture of any guns with barrels of the older-type of steel. Enough was on hand for the guns made with Damascus barrels for this period, after which only modern process steel was used. But improvements in the mechanism and design of double guns were in the offing, dictated by the mechanical advancements which had been growing up around the time of, and encouraged by, the war.

Parker, as always, was certainly not content to lag behind in the field of contemporary mechanical improvements, but, as always, was insistent on the highest possible quality and reliability in such improvements as it adopted. No catalogs issued by Parker during the twenties have come to light. This is strange, as the company most certainly issued them during the decade of improvements and much older catalogs seem to be at least available in small quantity. The lack of them is not a serious hinderance to a study of the gun's history, however, since the important improvements and additions to the Parker line are a matter of record. During the era of wonderful nonsense at least a half dozen outstanding firsts, as listed in the chapter on important Parker dates, had their origin.

In 1920 Fred Gilbert established the world's record with a Parker. In 1922 the single-trigger mechanism was introduced, in 1923 the first beaver-tail forearm, in 1926 the first ventilated rib ever used on a double gun, and in 1927 the first Parker in a 410 gauge. By 1928 the production figures reached 190,000 and by the last year of the decade, when production was running about 5000 guns a year, Parker could celebrate the production of its 200,000th shotgun in a very special way which will be described shortly.

All of the above improvements, no doubt listed successively in the catalogs published during the 1920's, are listed in the Parker catalog for January 1, 1930, the last year of the decade.

The 1930 Parker Catalog

The catalog issued on the eve of the fatal decade of the thirties reveals ten changes in the Parker line over what it had been in 1919, the eve of the preceding decade.

The first of the three is in the form of three deletions. First, as previously noted, all Damascus and/or twist steel barrels have been eliminated from the Parker line, the last shotgun with such barrels having been made about 1920. Second, the hammer mechanism has been dropped completely about the same time. Third, the P. grade gun has been discontinued. These deletions were a natural part of the evolution of the modern shotgun, but the very fact that Parker waited so long to make them is a tribute to both the gun's intrinsic quality and the conservatism of the firm.

Parker, however, was not looking at the question of gun design from a purely negative standpoint. While eliminating three aspects of the line, two of which went back to the first guns built, it was well aware of the necessity of keeping up to date with the latest improvements. In this connection the firm not only kept up to date but made its own contribution to the theory of gun design and the improvement of a gun's shooting qualities. The 1930 catalog offers the single-trigger mechanism, a raised matted rib and a beaver tail forearm, all of which were available for new guns ordered or for factory fitting to earlier models; all three improvements were available for any models except the Trojan.

In addition, the entire Parker line had by this time undergone four modifications, all of which further improved and modernized it. The first of these was the elimination of the plain extractor in favor of the automatic ejector mechanism in all but the lowest priced models, *ie.,* the D., G., V. and Trojan grades. The Parker Company had, as previously noted, released a .410 gauge gun for the first time in 1927; and the 1930 catalog offers the D., G., and V. grades in this bore.

The engraving designs on the higher grades show a change from what they were in the earlier catalogs, although this may be merely a matter of variation in advertising samples. It has been mentioned in the chapter on Special Features that on the higher grade guns the purchaser had the option of selecting his engraving from a variety of designs which the factory kept on hand for inspection or, if he so desired, of submitting a design or photo, possibly of his favorite dog. For this reason there is no doubt that at least a certain amount of variation exists among the various engraving scenes found on the higher-grade Parkers of any one year or period of manufacture.

In closing the analysis of the Parker line for 1930, it is necessary and fitting to add that the catalog for that year features one completely new and unique addition to the guns offered, and one which is not only another unique feature among so many others which marked and honored Parker history but one which constitutes the unique item of its kind in the firearms history of the United States. This outstanding and unequalled masterpiece of the gunmaker's art, craft and skill is pictured on the reverse side of the first page of the 1930 Parker catalog. Of all Parkers it deserves special comment and so will be discussed at the end of this chapter in the section on Special models.

The 1934 Parker Catalog

Coming to the last catalog issued by Parker as an independent concern, the pocket catalog dated January 1, 1934, there is but one difference to be noted in the entire line of guns and that only a mechanical variation. The economy model, the Trojan, is offered with the single trigger. Apparently, the factory had found it economically feasible to make this change in view of the fact that the Trojan constituted nearly half of its production total and that extended production of the single-trigger device had made the mechanism itself more economical to turn out. Prices in the 1930 and 1934 catalogs indicate that this was so. The company thus very well stabilized its entire line to a uniform variety of mechanical pattern and balanced prices only five months to the day before it bowed to the inevitable and became a subsidiary of the Remington Arms Company.

The Parker-Remington Folder for 1934

What is apparently the first brochure of any sort issued by Remington after it assumed control of Parker, a large and very attractive folder published sometime late in 1934, reveals no real difference or change from what the line had been on the first of that year. Exactly the same guns are offered but there is one variation and one important addition. All models, with the exception of the Trojan, are here offered only with automatic ejectors and all models, except the Trojan, are now available in a special skeet model. This particular model was the first of only two additions to the line which were made between the time Remington took over and the time manufacture of the gun ceased, the other one being a double-barrel trap model offered in the 1937 catalog.

The skeet special, as this model was called, was apparently most popular in the V. grade and is pictured in that particular grade in the last catalog issued by the company as well as catalogs of various dealers such as Stoeger. Once again, no change was made in the gun's quality or basic design and the new owners made no attempt whatever to alter traditional policy in any way. They sanctioned the addition of a gun specially made for a very popular shooting sport and the result was another outstanding Parker of which all too few were made. The general specifications of all other guns in the Parker line were, with the apparent elimination of the plain extractor, except in the Trojan, completely unchanged.

The 1937 Parker-Remington Catalog

In the year 1937 the last Parker catalog was issued and for the last catalog of America's finest shotgun the advertising division of Remington created and turned out what is certainly the most beautiful catalog ever published by an American gun maker. This final Parker catalog is, in fact, quite deserving of a special word of comment but I will reserve this for the chapter on buying and collecting Parkers.

As far as the Parker line itself is concerned, this Remington-Parker catalog, released in 1937 and issued until 1942 as the factory's standard presentation of what was available in Parkers, shows but three differences from the 1934 folder: the factory is now making a double-barrel Trap Gun; the D., G. and V. grades are once again offered with plain extractor if the purchaser wishes this instead of the automatic ejector; and all models except the Trojan are offered in .410 gauge. In commenting on the modification and addition of the double-barrel Trap Model, one is again led to observe that Parker, under direction of Remington, is still responsive to the demands of the shooting public; and, during these last years of the gun's manufacture in the 1930's, is attempting to give the shooters what they want in Parker quality.

In this connection, it should be remembered that trap shooting had become extremely popular by the late twenties and early thirties and that double-barrel guns designed especially for this sport were more in demand than ever before. So it is not surprising that, exactly twenty years after the famous single-barrel trap gun had been introduced in 1917, Parker turned out its first double gun of this type. It was an immediate success but, as in the case of the skeet gun, there was such a short time left for Parkers to be made only a fairly small number of this model was actually produced.

The fact that in 1937 all the shotguns except the economy model were available for order in .410 gauge is certainly an unmistakable reflection of the popularity which this little load enjoyed during the thirties. It will be remembered that the 1930 and 1934 catalogs had offered .410 guns only in the lowest of the standard grades —D., G. and V. The 1934 Remington folder makes no mention of the gauges of the guns offered but it is safe to assume that the new owners and the factory technicians had not found reason to offer practically the entire line in .410, as soon as the company changed hands. The fact that they did make this decision by 1937, only three years later, is certainly an interesting indication, as just observed, of the popularity the .410 had attained at this time. The explanation for this widespread demand for guns chambered for it seems, by today's standards, difficult to find and is certainly all the more elusive when considered in relation to the most expensive shotguns made in the United States.

I think this explanation may be found in several facts about the general sport of shooting as it had come to be enjoyed in all of North America by the 1930's. At that time more persons of both sexes and all ages were going in for shooting than ever before in the history of Canada, the United States and Mexico. This, in turn, was the result of several factors: guns had played a big part in the founding of all three nations and the topography of all three had always offered unequaled opportunities for hunting; the first World War had, indirectly at least, encouraged hunting as it had all other forms of shooting; the society which grew up in the United States in particular during the roaring twenties, with its emphasis on the country club and sports as a genteel and socially respectable mode of recreation, naturally encouraged more shooting; the complete equality of women, finally made part of the Constitution by the Nineteenth Amendment, resulted in more women going out for what had previously been almost exclusively male sports.

It is in this participation by women and young persons of both sexes that a large part of the .410's popularity is to be found. Shooters in both groups having any need for a shotgun naturally turned to the bore having the mildest report and recoil. Of course, the .410 gauge had always been popular with youngsters and had, since the late nineteenth century, been widely available in low-priced single-barrel shotguns as well as in some of the commoner doubles. The widening of the shooting public to include more financially well-off enthusiasts than ever before, many of whom were women, naturally created a greater demand for high quality .410 guns.

In addition, the improvement of the shell itself had made the small bore definitely something more than a toy or training gun. The .410 started with a length of only two inches (a size still quite common in Europe today), increased to $2\frac{1}{2}$ by the 1920's, and finally was improved and modernized in the 3 inch size by the mid 1930's. This three inch .410 gauge load contributed much to the popularity enjoyed by the guns of this bore during Parker's last years. Of course, all of this seems a bit strange to us of the fifties. Now, women commonly shoot .12 and .16 gauge guns and the .20 gauge in a light field load is considered quite suitable even for a teenage girl. This change in preference comes from an acceptance of heavier gauge shotguns by women, who, by the time of the Second World War and after, had gotten over to a large extent, their traditional fear of standard-sized loads.

It is interesting to note that America's great shotgun authority of the past generation, Major Charles Askins, remarked in his book, *Modern Shotguns and Loads* that, while he understood the appeal the .410 gauge had for women and young people, he personally regarded it as of little value for practical shotgun shooting and that whenever he saw a full-grown man carrying one into the woods for serious hunting, he always had the feeling that nature had made a mistake in the man's sex. Whatever we may think of the .410 shell's practical value today (and some excellent guns are still made for it) the Parkers of this gauge, made during the last fifteen years of the company's history, and in high grades only during the last five, constitute what is without doubt one of the rarest categories of America's premier shotgun.

The fact that the 1937 catalog again offers the plain extractor instead of the automatic ejector in the D., G., and V. grades, probably does not indicate that this feature had been entirely withdrawn from these guns in 1934. The Remington folder for that year simply does not make any mention of any guns but the ejector type. It is unlikely that the factory would have discontinued the extractor and then revised it so soon even in lower grade guns. The 1934 folder does not give all the details a catalog would almost necessarily give so it probably just failed to mention that the extractor could still be had in prefence to the ejector on the lower grade shotguns. The 1937 Catalog offers it only on special order, indicating that the factory had all but discontinued it as a part of the Parker mechanism.

The last catalog of Parker shotguns, coming out in one of the last years of fairly stable world conditions.

THE PARKER GUN

"C. H. E." GRADE

Selected best grade walnut stock and fore-end, hand bored checkered. Sterling silver name plate inlaid in stock. Stock with any specifications desired, including cheek piece, Monte Carlo or cast off, and any style of grip. Rubber recoil pad or skeleton steel butt plate. Engraving in game scenes and scroll. Nickel plated triggers. Ivory sights if desired. Automatic ejectors. Made in 10, 12, 16, 20, 28 and .410 gauges. Any boring of barrels. See page 8 for weights, barrel lengths, chamber lengths, and other specifications; for maximum long range 12 ga. and 10 ga. guns; and page 7 for selection of gun cases.

	Net*	Wholesale*	Retail*
"C. H. E." Grade with double triggers	$197.73	$219.56	$290.00
"C. H. E." Grade with selective single trigger	219.55	243.70	322.00
Beavertail fore-end, extra	17.95	21.25	25.00
Raised ventilated rib, extra	23.86	29.75	35.00
Extra set of interchangeable barrels, including regular fore-end	115.84	135.20	148.00

"D. H. E." GRADE

Stock and fore-end of fancy walnut, finely hand checkered. Sterling silver name plate inlaid in stock. Stock custom-built to any specifications desired without extra charge, including cheek piece, Monte Carlo or cast off, and any style of grip. Rubber recoil pad or skeleton steel butt plate. Engraving is game scenes and scroll. Nickel plated triggers. Ivory sights if desired. Automatic ejectors. Made in 10, 12, 16, 20, 28, and .410 gauges. Any boring of barrels. See page 8 for weights, barrel lengths, chamber lengths, and other specifications; for maximum long range 12 ga. and 10 ga. guns; and page 7 for selection of gun cases.

	Net*	Wholesale*	Retail*
"D. H. E." Grade with double triggers	$132.95	$163.75	$195.00
"D. H. E." Grade with selective single trigger	154.77	192.50	227.00
Beavertail fore-end, extra	12.95	16.15	19.00
Raised ventilated rib, extra	20.45	25.50	30.00
Extra set of interchangeable barrels, including regular fore-end	85.40	99.00	119.00

*EXCISE TAX INCLUDED
*U. S. EXCISE TAX OF 10% TO BE ADDED

A page from the jobber's confidential price list stamped thereon, "Effective July 1, 1940. The U. S. Excise Tax has been increased from 10% to 11%, therefore 11% should be added to prices shown herein."

is a fitting public close to the career of America's finest shotgun. It offered, in the most luxuriously printed gun catalog ever offered in the United States, the largest line of shotguns, and all of top quality, ever offered by any gunmaker.

The Parker-Remington 1940 Jobber's Price List

While the beautiful 1937 Catalog was the last general description and offering of the Parker line made to the public, during the succeeding five years that the gun was in general production the Sales and Executive Offices of Remington issued Confidential Jobber's Price Lists describing and picturing the entire Parker line as well as giving net, wholesale and retail prices. As far as can be determined, the last one of these Jobber's Price Lists issued by Remington is that dated February 16, 1940. This list, in the form of an eight page booklet, pictures and details the full line of Parker guns and accessories offered at that time. The prices were no doubt raised by about ten percent after the outbreak of war in December 1941, at least on the lower-priced models, but the contents of the folder are significant as the last official offering of the Parker line in any form before manufacture of the gun ceased entirely.

And the Parker line, as it was made during the last year before the United States entered World War II and for a time afterwards, is, with two exceptions, exactly the same as that offered in the 1937 catalog. These two exceptions are a complete discontinuance of the plain-extractor feature on all guns and the discontinuance of one particular model—the Trojan. The first of these two final changes in the line is not at all surprising; it is, rather, only to be expected in view of the steady if slow modernization of the mechanism down through the years. The final complete elimination of the plain extractor was the logical outcome of the general trend toward the utmost in modern improvement which the double gun had been undergoing since the late 1870's when it was first brought out in a hammerless form. The automatic ejector mechanism was, like most innovations in mechanical design, first offered as an option with the older design which naturally had its adherents for many years to come.

The financial aspect of the matter was also a determining factor, since in the beginning, the automatic-ejector feature was priced at from $25.00 to $35.00 over the price of a gun with the plain extractor. The 1912 catalog had offered the entire line with or without the ejector. The 1915 line eliminated the extractor in the very high grades; the 1917 line eliminated it in still more of the higher grades, and the 1930, 1934 and 1937 lines offered it only for the least expensive models. In the Trojan the ejector was never offered at all.

By the late thirties, the economic picture had changed to such an extent that elimination of the extractor was no doubt economically advisable. The country was out of the depression, the economy was picking up, especially with preparations for war. The average shooter did not find $25.00 or so such an abnormally higher price to pay for such a convenience as the automatic ejector. Such a sum had, in fact, by that time become a matter of no real difference at all to anyone who could afford what was in 1940 still an expensive gun even in the lower-priced models. In its last models made, the Parker line fully exemplified the most modern and up-to-date design in a double gun.

The reasons for the second change in the final offering of Parkers to the public, the elimination of the Trojan, are much less apparent. Such a decision by the factory actually seems almost inexplicable in view of this economy gun's popularity. The Trojan had, since its introduction in 1915, been the largest seller in the Parker line, at least 40 percent of each subsequent year's production total having been allocated to it.

But the Trojan was gone by 1940 and seems to have been actually dropped from the line in 1939. This latter fact is evidenced by the great Stoeger Arms catalogs for the fall of 1938 and 1939. The catalog for the former year features it prominently; the one for the latter year neither pictures nor mentions it. The company which, above all others in the United States, made it an absolute must to have everything in guns in the United States, from a $.25 water pistol to the Parker A-1 Special in its catalog, would hardly have failed to offer so popular a gun had it been still available.

The explanation may very well lie, again, in the change in economic conditions which had taken place in North America since the depression and which had vastly increased the buying power of so many Americans by the late thirties. In the 1939 catalog Stoeger lists the Parker V.H.E. at $125.00, presumably the factory stipulated retail price since Stoeger never gave discounts or used sale prices in catalogs. The last price listed for the Trojan is $72.50 in the Stoeger 1938 Catalog. It may be that the factory, since passing under the control of Remington, found that it was economically unsound to market an economy-grade firearm when it was the only one in so large a line of otherwise very expensive guns.

True, the Trojan had been a big seller but its greatest sales had been in years where its price was far lower than 1938 ($55.00 in 1930) and when the buying power of the American dollar and the American public were nothing like what they were in 1939. In addition, by 1939 prices were on the rise, wages had increased, and a factory whose sole double gun was a handmade shotgun, with every refinement of design and superiority of action, no doubt found it more profitable to concentrate solely on a line which featured basically the same design and mechanical structure in the guns offered. The difference in price between the V. and Trojan, about $40.00 in 1938, had no doubt become by 1939 too little to make any real difference to anyone ready to spend over $80.00 for a shotgun. So, as in the case of the plain extractor and the automatic ejector, the economy item, rendered unnecessary by the state of the nation's economy, was dropped in favor of a more unified line in which all items were of a relatively expensive sort.

The Parker Jobber's Price List of February 16, 1940, also has some interesting accessory items listed in relation to the gun itself and convenience in the use of it. Every gun in the line is offered, at the standard retail price, with standard sighting plane and double triggers. But every gun is also available with selective single trigger, beaver-tail fore-end, a raised ventilated rib and an extra set of interchangeable barrels, including a regular fore-end. Prices for these extras are shown in the illustrations and in the appendices. This price list also features, on its last page, three types of cases for shotguns: a full-length, sheepskin-lined case; an English mutton-leg case; and the finest trunk-type case. The last one is offered as custom built only in heavy tan or black top grain cowhide on bass wood, with high-grade handle, brass fittings, green billiard cloth lining, compartment for cleaning equipment, and, where ordered, a compartment for extra barrels.

In the last years of that restless unpredictable, surprising decade of the thirties the final line of Parker Guns, produced under the auspices of Remington, still maintained the solidarity, variety, quality and uniformity which had always characterized Parker and which would shortly, with the coming of World War II, become only a memory.

General Specifications of the Parker Line

When we come to consider the general specifications of Parker guns, we are at once faced with a very large number of figures which deal with every dimension of a gun. In this connection it is necessary to again remember the controlling fact of all Parker production: all guns made by the factory, from the time the shotgun was well-developed, were custom built. There were of course always inventory guns in stock, these being made to the specifications which had proved to be most generally in demand. There was, however, absolutely no deviation in quality from the guns made to strictly custom orders in which the purchaser could select any specification he desired. It is this catering to individual orders for so long a period of time which makes a breakdown of Parker specifications so difficult to accomplish. It is quite possible to locate a Parker in almost any combination of design one wishes—at least there is a good possibility that any design which appeals to the prospective buyer was at one time made. To this must be added the fact that, as in the case of any product made to custom order, many specimens were turned out with very odd, unusual or even freakish features. The factory was anxious to take care of any orders which could be filled without compromising the quality of the gun. So it can be always assumed that any Parker, regardless of the specifications, was never made in such a way as to impair the gun's traditional standards.

The general facts about Parker design can be fairly well summarized and they provide a good chart for the entire line.

Pistol grip: All Parkers, except the Trojan, were available with full-pistol grip, half-pistol grip or straight stock. It seems to be the experience of most gun enthusiasts that Parkers with straight stocks are rare or seldom found. The writer of this book has only seen two such guns in his lifetime, but it should be emphasized that this is no definite indication as to the number actually produced. Straight-grip double guns have never been as popular in the United States as in Europe and the design in general has always been produced in smaller numbers than the full- and half-pistol grips.

Butt Plates: Parker stocks were made with four types of butt finish: Skeleton steel, checkered wood, hard rubber and soft rubber recoil pad. The skeleton steel plate is most often found on the higher grades, from D. on up. The grades from D. down were offered with either checkered wood or hard rubber. The hard-rubber butt plates were often made with the head of a dog carrying a bird in its mouth with the name Parker just above. The Trojan butt plate is always of hard rubber with milled surface. The soft-rubber recoil pads were not introduced as a standard part of the gun's equipment until the late twenties or early thirties. In the last

Parker catalogs they are prominently displayed.

Stocks: Stock dimensions were available to any specifications the purchaser desired but those which deviated from the factory standard were priced higher on the lower grade guns. The regular drops were from 2 to 3¼ inches. The regular lengths were from 13½ to 14½ inches. Any stocks which were not within these dimensions required extra handwork for which there was an extra charge of ten dollars on guns of V. to C. grades inclusive. Monte Carlo stocks or stocks with cheek pieces were also available on special order for all models and the same charge was made for these deviations in the V. to C. grades as for any change in measurements.

Barrel lengths: The Parker Shotgun was made in a variety of barrel lengths from about 24 to 40 inches. The most frequently-found lengths are naturally the standard ones popular in double guns—26, 28, 30, 32 and 34 inches, the last being often used on the trap models. It is rare to see a Parker of fairly modern vintage (except the trap guns) with a barrel length of more than 32 inches. The older guns were much more often made with unusually long barrels because of the popularity of such barrels for long-range bird shooting at a time when black powder was universally used and even for a time after the introduction of the smokeless type.

The Parker catalogs up to 1917 offer guns in barrel lengths ranging from 24 to 40 inches. The 40 inch length, however, was offered only for 8, 10 and 12 gauge guns and then at an extra charge. By 1930 barrels of more than 34 inches had been dropped from the line, the factory declining to accept any orders for barrels shorter than 24 inches or exceeding 34 inches. Even then an extra charge was made if the length was not usually made for a gun of the gauge which the customer ordered. From 1934 on, the standard barrel lengths were 26, 28, 30, 32 and 34 inches, the last still being usually made only for trap guns. Barrel lengths other than these and for any gun were still offered and remained available to the end of the gun's existence. The minimum length was kept at 24 inches and the maximum at 34, with the extra charges also retained for making barrels for any size gun for which the particular length was not customarily made.

Gauges: In the course of its life span, the Parker was made in 8, 10, 12, 14, 16, 20, 28 and .410 gauge.

Although the 8 gauge was offered up to about 1917, few guns were actually made in this large bore after 1900. The greater ballistic power of smokeless powder, better choke design of gun barrels and stricter hunting laws regulating the size of weapons all combined to make giant-size shotguns impractical.

The 10 gauge remained in the line from the earliest years until the last Parkers were made, although here again the actual number of 10 gauge guns manufactured was, at least by the time of the First World War, comparatively small. One of the most eagerly-sought Parkers in the 10 gauge size is that chambered for the 10 gauge magnum shell in a $3\frac{1}{2}$ inch chamber. The exact number of these big magnums made by Parker is not possible to determine. The fact that they were sold only on special, non-cancellable order, however, is sufficient indication that the number was small.[1]

The 12 gauge, as one might expect, was the most

---

[1] This is especially probable when we consider the fact that Ithaca, the only American gun maker to specialize in modern 10 gauge magnum doubles, made only 998 in a period of some ten years.

popular size Parker and more of them were made than any other bore. The 3 inch magnum chamber was also available for this size on special order and a much larger number of 12 gauge magnums were turned out than those of 10 gauge.

The 14 gauge was an intermediate-size shell which was popular only until around the time of the First World War and for which few guns were manufactured even before then. It is today regarded as something of a freak and the reason for its ever being made is a bit elusive. The explanation is probably to be found in the fact that, when black powder made quite a ballistic difference in the performance of shotgun shells and shooters were used to a large variety of shells of all sizes and types, a finer graduation in bore sizes seemed to be desirable. In any case, Parker offered the 14 gauge until 1917, but only in grades G. and P.

The 16 and 20 gauge guns were naturally the most popular of the smaller sizes in which the Parker came and all grades were made in these bores as in the 12, from the A-1 Special to the Trojan.

The 28 gauge is of special interest in the history of the Parker, since it was Parker who first developed and marketed a gun of this size. From 1903, when the first .28 gauge gun was produced, all grades were offered in this bore except the Trojan. Despite the fact that this would seem to indicate that there are many 28 gauge Parkers in circulation, the exact reverse of this is apparently true; it is somewhat rare to find a 28 gauge Parker and the majority of them were probably made in the higher grades.

The same is true, but in even larger measure, of the .410 gauge. Parker did not manufacture guns of this small bore until 1927 and the number made before the gun was discontinued was very small. A .410 gauge Parker is a rare item indeed.

It is entirely possible that, before the turn of the century, some Parkers were made in very odd sizes, such as 6 and 24 gauges. The factory was doing custom work that had as yet not been standardized into a definite line, so orders for such freakish bores might have been accepted. The exact facts about these odd pieces, if they existed at all, cannot be determined.

Boring: Parkers were made in all bores and combinations of bores. Even the Trojan, on which no deviations from the standard specifications were accepted, was offered with any combination of bores the customer desired, provided he placed a special order. Boring could be had from true cylinder to extreme full choke. The general practice of the factory was, however, to make up inventory guns and special-order guns where no boring was specified, with the right barrel bored modified choke and the left barrel bored full choke. This did not apply, of course, to guns made for Skeet and Trap shooting, guns for the former type being made with the regular skeet bore and those of the latter with full choke.

Weights: The weight of a Parker gun depended, as does that of any shotgun, on its gauge, general design, and barrel length. Parkers were offered from 5⅞ lbs. in a .410 gauge with 26 inch barrels to 11 lbs. in a 10 gauge magnum with 32 inch barrels. In the older guns, when the 8 gauge was still being made and Damascus barrels used, the weight could total as much as 14 pounds and guns of this now almost-unbelievable weight were still offered in 1915. Since the weight of a shotgun is, to a large extent, dependent on the length of the barrels, it is to be expected that Parkers with barrels of unusual length will total an unusually heavy weight. It could very well be possible, for instance, that if, back in 1908 or 1910, a hunter wanting real long range shooting and not afraid of a heavy load, had ordered his Parker in 10 gauge bore with 40 inch Damascus steel barrels' his piece would have weighed nearly fifteen pounds.

Chamber Lengths: Parker guns were made in chamber lengths of from 2¾ inches to 3½ inches. The longest chambers were naturally made for magnum shells and were made only on special order, in 3 inch for the 12 gauge magnum and 3½ inch for 10 gauge magnum.

Parker seems always to have produced its guns with standard length chambers. The earliest catalogs available list nothing shorter than what is considered standard today and the old Parker brass shells of the 1870's and 1880's indicate that in those decades the Parker chamber was not intended for short shells.

Finally, it should be observed that all guns in the Parker line, with the sole exception of the Trojan, were made with a quick-removal device for the fore-end. This took the form of a lever with a curved top, mounted in a recessed half-sphere. A flick of the forefinger was all that was necessary to remove the fore-end, thus effecting complete take-down of the entire gun in a matter of seconds.

Special Models

The consideration of the Parker line may properly close with an examination of a half-dozen special types of shotguns, each of which is an outstanding model of its own type and which possesses features of special interest to the student and collector of American or for that matter any kind of shotguns. Of course, it may be logically presumed that, by this point, the reader is quite fully aware that the Parker as a gun is indeed special; that the entire line was originated and maintained as something very special, namely, the finest shotgun it was humanly possible to produce. Within the Parker line, however, there were from time to time new additions or unique productions which are of sufficient value and interest to demand individual consideration.

The first such Parker to necessitate separate comment is the line's economy model, the Trojan. This, not without good reason, was, as previously indicated, by far the company's best-selling shotgun. From its introduction in 1915, when it sold for $27.50, to the last year it was made, 1939, when the retail price was $72.50, the Trojan made up at least 40 percent of each year's total production. It is thus the particular Parker which, at the present time, is most often found in gun stores. In considering the Trojan, it is interesting to note that this strictly economy gun was not introduced until the Parker Company had been in business for some forty-seven years. The explanation for this long delay in marketing a low-priced arm is that, at a time when a very large number of American firms were making cheap doubles selling for as little as ten dollars new and other firms were turning out both good and poor quality weapons, Parker had never attempted the production of anything but strictly first class guns. In the days before the First World War, when finances created a type of purchasing power very different from that of our day, a firm whose product had been always intended for wealthy patrons or those willing to spend an amount far above the average for a gun, found no possible necessity or justification for attempting a low-priced gun.

In addition, it is necessary to remember that, before the Trojan's introduction, the general process of gun manufacture would have made it very difficult, if not impossible for a firm whose only product was a top-grade weapon to produce an economy grade consistent with the quality Parker had always demanded in all its products.

By the start of the first great war, however, American purchasing power had increased and engineering methods developed to the point where an economy gun of the quality demanded by Parker was possible. This was helped by the general shift from Damascus to modern steel, making possible the production of gun barrels of reasonably high tensile strength selling for a low price. In any case, the Parker Trojan certainly fulfilled all the company's expectations—a fact well evidenced by its consistent popularity across the years. And, in addition, it certainly lived up to the company's demand for quality in the cheapest gun. The Trojan is without a doubt the finest economy grade shotgun ever produced in the United States and probably anywhere in the world. And it is still, in a good used model, the best buy in a shotgun on the American market.

The differences between the Trojan and other Parker models, which made it possible to produce it at a low price, have been indicated in the historical survey of the Parker line. It was made to standard specifications only. The only choices allowed in placing an order were in the matter of choke, barrel length and trigger mechanism, and it was not until after Parker had been making it for about fifteen years that a choice of boring was allowed or that it was offered with the single trigger. The Trojan was never available in any size but the popular 12, 16 and 20 gauges. It was not made with an automatic ejector or beaver tail forearm. It was never offered in the trap or skeet model and no engraving or decoration was ever used anywhere on it. The stock and forearm were of a lower quality wood than that used in the rest of the line but one which was absolutely dependable. Also, these parts were not as richly finished as they were on the other Parkers, even those of lower price. No grip cap was put on the Trojan's stock which was made with full pistol grip only, and the butt plate was always of hard, milled rubber.

Although a recoil pad was available at extra charge, another refinement of design lacking on the Trojan, one found in every other gun in the Parker line, was the quick removal device on the fore-arm. In order to be sure that this important part of the gun would not jar off or be knocked off easily, the fore-arm hinge on the Trojan is unusually tight. Once put on, the fore-arm is really on to stay until the user has serious reason for removing it. Nothing will disengage it. Removing the fore-arm of a Parker Trojan requires a long, steady, very determined application of pressure from both thumbs just under the tip. In fact, to one unacquainted with the process this can prove downright discouraging.

It is generally best not to attempt to take the Trojan apart except for special reasons, such as packing it or shipping it. This really isn't necessary for proper cleaning, and the sturdy construction renders any kind of mechanical complications almost impossible. In the event that it is necessary to take down a Trojan, however, proceed cautiously and *never* attempt to use any form of tool or implement to pry the fore-arm loose. Both the under-tip of this piece, and more important, the barrels, will certainly be marred, perhaps to the point of no return. Unless you have very powerful and well-exercised thumbs, the best way to remove the fore-arm of a Trojan is as follows: place the gun, bottom up, on a couch or divan, with the butt firmly against the end of the couch's arm rest. Then press very hard against the tip until you feel it give a little. A slight increase in pressure will then dislodge it. When it is necessary to put the gun back together, the fore-arm can be easily snapped into place by a quick pressure of the hand around the barrels.

The mechanism of the later Trojan models lacks one part found on other Parkers—the barrel extension lug which makes the closing of the breech tighter and surer. This, however, does not detract from the gun's safety in any way as the bolting system, as previously described, is so sure and tight that the gun could be fired with the top lever open and still not come open at the breech. It is very interesting to note that this extension lug was a feature of the Trojan from the time that it was introduced up until some time in the 1920's and that the barrels, in the first models, were given a plain black finish, while during the 1930's and possibly before the same rich, dark browning process was used on Trojan barrels as on those of all other Parkers. Why the one feature was dropped and the other added is something of a mystery. It may be that changes in the general process of manufacture rendered the barrel lug more expensive than was deemed practical for such a grade of gun and that the browning process by the 1930's came to be more of a factor in increasing the Trojan's cost than the absence of it would have reduced the cost.

The frame of the Trojan was, at least in the years

following the first World War, always case hardened. As in the case of the V. grade, this process added beauty, durability and resistance to scratching to the gun's overall quality and appearance.

The design of the Trojan lacks one feature which characterizes every other gun in the Parker line: it does not have the graceful curved shoulders in the front part of the frame which constitute a large part of the Parker's classical beauty of form. The straight lines add a certain plainness of outline which takes something away from the gun's appearance but was certainly an important factor in reducing its cost, because much less attention and shaping was required to produce a frame of this model's design than those used in other Parkers.

However, the Trojan was offered as an economy gun and that is what it always remained; so the lack of refinement was not an important factor in the average shooter's reaction to it. In 1939, the last year in which this model was made, its selling price of almost eighty dollars was a very high one in comparison to the low prices of so many doubles for sale in the United States. This was at a time when the American dollar was worth all of its one hundred cents and eighty of them could purchase quite a lot of quality in a firearm. It would take, at the present time, from three to four times the price of the last Trojans made to produce one of equal quality, if indeed such quality were capable of present achievement at all.

The quality and value of the Parker Trojan lie in precisely those aspects which made Parker the nation's finest shotgun: finest workmanship, expert attention to detail and hand finishing throughout. The Trojan, like all Parkers, was a hand-made, hand-finished gun with

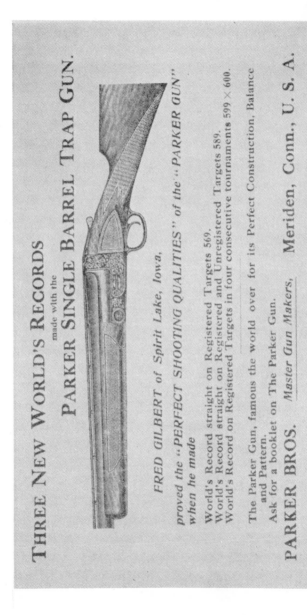

THREE NEW WORLD'S RECORDS
made with the
PARKER SINGLE BARREL TRAP GUN.

FRED GILBERT of Spirit Lake, Iowa,

proved the "PERFECT SHOOTING QUALITIES" of the "PARKER GUN" when he made

World's Record straight on Registered Targets 569.
World's Record straight on Registered and Unregistered Targets 589.
World's Record on Registered Targets in four consecutive tournaments 599 × 600.

The Parker Gun, famous the world over for its Perfect Construction, Balance and Pattern.
Ask for a booklet on The Parker Gun.

PARKER BROS.   *Master Gun Makers,*   **Meriden, Conn., U. S. A.**

A mailing card advertising the Parker Single Barrel Trap Gun.

every bit as much personal care exercised in the making of it as in other Parkers and regulated for the strongest and most modern loads. It was Parker's only economy gun and as such was the kind of economy gun only Parker could build.

The Parker Single Barrel Trap Gun

The design and production of a single barrel trap gun as the one and only exception to its one-type line of guns gave Parker Brothers, in 1917, the lead over all other makers of American shotguns as well as an almost instantaneous primacy in trap shooting records. There were, to be sure, many other American companies making shotguns in 1917—a fact previously indicated. But no American gun maker then in business had previously marketed so high a grade single-barrel shot gun designed exclusively for the then rather exclusive sport of Trap Shooting. Many records had been made in the past with double guns and repeaters; in the case of the latter type the famous old Winchester Model 97 pump gun had given a particularly fine account of itself in the hands of men like the well-known Browning Brothers of Ogden, Utah. The use of a single-barrel gun for top-flight trap shooting, however, was an idea which American gun makers were just beginning to accept around the time of the First World War. Parker, always conscious of the public's need in the gun line, could here safely consider what seemed to be a plausible innovation in both its own and the nation's line of shotguns. The mechanism for the single-barrel shotgun could easily be developed in a factory specializing in double-barrel guns and could even more easily be made to a high standard of quality, the single-trigger mechanism, perforce, being of less complex structure than that of the double trigger. Furthermore, the single-barrel gun was capable of just as much custom designing and fine quality finishing as a double and was therefore one with which Parker could put all of its traditional standards with complete assurance of making a top quality gun of superior shooting qualities.

Once again, the cautious conservatism of Parker engineers paid off. The Parker Single-Barrel Trap Gun is without doubt the finest gun of its kind every turned out in this part of the world and made the greatest scores in the trap shooting field. It rivals or outclasses even the fine English and European guns of a similar type. Anyone who has ever had the experience of handling this superb shotgun will testify that the very feel of it puts confidence into the shooter. It was available, like the Parker Double Guns, in a series of grades on an ascending scale of quality from SC to SA-1 Special, the

A tiny receiver presumably made by an employee of the factory and discovered at a later time by Charles S. Parker, last president of the firm, when the building was cleared out prior to removal of all machinery to Ilion after Remington purchased the company. Photo made by Leo J. Gallenstein.

finish and workmanship on each model corresponding in quality with the similar grade double guns.

Parker offered the Single Barrel Trap Gun in 12 gauge only for 2¾ inch shells. The barrel could be had in 30, 32 or 34 inch length and was regularly bored full choke, although any other boring could be had by special order. All models were made with ventilated rib, beaver-tail fore-end, automatic ejector and Hawkins soft rubber recoil pad. Any other make of pad was also available. The stock and fore-end could of course be had to any reasonable dimensions and were made to the customer's order. The stock was regularly made with full pistol grip and rubber cap, with dimensions of 14⅜ inches long including the recoil pad, 1⅞ inches drop at heel, and 1½ inches drop at comb. The option of any other stock dimensions included cheek piece, Monte Carlo or cast-off and straight or half pistol grip all without extra charge.

Parker, in making a single barrel trap gun, followed the same course that all other American makes of double guns had followed or were to follow within the next five years. By 1922, all five makers of America's finest double shotguns had two things in common: with the exception of a single-barrel trap gun each company made only double-barred guns; and the single-barrel trap gun in each line was a high quality piece in every way. In 1917, when the Parker Single-Barrel Trap Gun was produced, Fox, the company's nearest rival, was not offering one. In 1922, however, Parker, Fox, Ithaca, L. C. Smith and even the old Baker Gun Company of Batavia, New York, all had a gun of this type in the catalog. The last-named company's product was known as The Elite and it was a handsome and beautiful gun, as was the Ithaca of this type. But no American company before 1917 had produced a Single Trap Gun of the quality of Parker's SA-1 Special. Before this date, in fact, foreign guns like the Francotte from Belgium had pretty well held the field for this kind of shooting both here and abroad. But Parker, as she had nearly forty years earlier in the case of the double-barrel gun, gave the United States top rank in the making of single barrel trap guns.

The Parker Double Barrel Trap Gun

Quite satisfied with the excellent scores and high popularity of the trap model with single barrel, the Parker Company did not offer a double barrel trap model until its very last years. This does not appear until the 1937 catalog and thus it was only developed some time between 1934 and 1937.

The double-barrel gun for trap shooting was analogous in many ways to the single barrel. It was available in all grades of the full double line from V. to A-1 special. It came regularly with selective single trigger and, like the single barrel model, was made with beaver tail fore-end, raised ventilated rib, and in 12 gauge only for $2\frac{3}{4}$ inch shells. There was also, as in the case of the single-barrel gun, an option of any barrel length or boring, the regular specifications being 30 or 32 inch barrels, both bored full choke. The optional design included non-automatic or automatic safety, ivory-bead or red-bead front sights, Hawkins or any other make of recoil pad, and any kind of stock grip. The regular stock dimensions were $14\frac{3}{8}$ inches long including recoil pad, $1\frac{7}{8}$ inches drop at heel, $1\frac{1}{2}$ inches drop at comb, but with option of any others including cheek piece, Monte-Carlo, or cast-off furnished in accordance with the specifications for these items according to the grade in which the gun was ordered.

The fact that the double-barrel trap gun was made in all grades of the full line of Parker doubles (except the Trojan) would at first lead one to imagine that a good many more of these were made and thus are available than the single-barrel trap gun. But the exact opposite of this is apparently true and the explanation is easy to find. Although the single-barrel trap gun was only made in five grades, starting with Grade C., it was put on the market at least eighteen years before the double trap gun and so there was ample time for many more of them to be made. The double-trap model was only made for a maximum period of seven years and possibly not that long. The number, in comparison with all other models, would have to be small and when the cost of the guns and the smaller shooting public in the second half of the 1930's are taken into consideration, the small number of these guns made is easily accounted for. The Parker Double-Barrel Trap Gun was made during the last half-dozen years of the gun's existence and was developed shortly after Remington took over in 1934. It was thus the last model added to the line before all manufacture of the gun in any form ceased. As the final model to bear the honored name of Parker, this shotgun, made for a comparatively very short time and then in fairly small quantity, is now a scarce item indeed and is very seldom offered for sale.

The Parker Skeet Gun

The skeet model was also a fairly late addition to the Parker line. It was, in fact, the next-to-the-last Parker developed, coming in 1934, just after Remington purchased the company and first appearing in the folder issued by Remington late in that year. It is, therefore, with the double-barrel trap gun, one of the only two Parkers actually added to the line after the company ceased operations as an independent firm. The probability is, however, that the development of the skeet gun had been underway for at least a time before the firm sold out, as the time between the last Parker catalog and the first Remington-Parker folder (less than six months) was too short to permit the offering of such a carefully-built precision product.

The Parker Skeet Gun, as a type of specialized shotgun, could be built in any grade; so it was, like the double barrel trap model, offered in all grades from VHE to A-1 Special. A checkered butt was supplied on the VHE and GHE grades and a skeleton steel butt plate on the DHE through A-1 Special grades. The weight and balance of the skeet gun were available to the customer's individual requirements. Parker made a point of offering the skeet model in a variety of gauges and weights and was prepared to make up several of different gauges so that they weighed in such a way that the swing, "feel" and balance of all would be the same.

The Parker Skeet Gun was regularly supplied with automatic ejectors, beavertail fore-end, non-automatic safety, and a selective single trigger. A ventilated rib was available at extra charge. It could be had in 12, 16, 20 and .410 gauges. The barrels were ordinarily supplied in 26 inch length bored for skeet shooting. This meant that the right barrel was marked "SKEET-OUT" for outgoing targets and the left marked "SKEET-IN" for the incomers. For those who preferred otherwise, however, there was an option of any other barrel length and boring. Both front and rear sights were of the ivory-bead type. The usual stock dimensions were 14 inches long, $2\frac{1}{4}$ inch drop at the heel and $1\frac{1}{2}$ inches drop at the comb, but here also the measurements could be made up to any reasonable special order. The general quality of the Skeet Gun's finish, involving the quality of the wood, the type of engraving and other features were commensurate with the quality of the grade in which it was ordered.

The only Parker publications to picture the skeet gun, and there were three of them (1934 folder, 1937 catalog and 1940 price list) show it in the VHE grade. This is the grade also shown in the catalogs of such large gun dealers as Stoeger, Abercrombie and Fitch, Von Lengerke and Antoine, etc. From the numbers of Parker Skeet Guns which show up in current use and are offered for sale, it appears that the majority were actually made in this grade. The fact that the Skeet model is so often seen indicates that at least a fair number were turned out in the eight years it was made. Parker had waited a long time to develop a Skeet gun and when it finally got around to doing so the product was in the finest traditions of the firm and its controlling standard of excellence.

The Parker "Try Gun"

A most unusual and all but unknown Parker gun was the so-called "try gun." This interesting shotgun was designed so that its dimensions were adjustable to a large extent. Never made available for public purchase, its purpose was to provide dealers serving a large number of persons with a very handy and practical gun device for calculating exactly the dimensions best suited to a

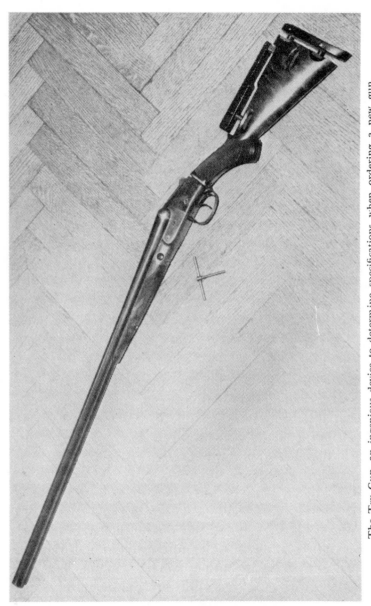

The Try Gun, an ingenious device to determine specifications when ordering a new gun.

prospective buyer. In the hands of a trained gunsmith or salesman, which Parker always endeavoured to secure for the sale of its guns, the try gun was an invaluable help in determining, in a few minutes, the measurements necessary for a buyer's special order for a Parker.

Although this device is never used in the United States today and is, in fact, completely unknown to a large segment of the shooting public, it is still quite commonly used in England by that country's master gun builders. The reasons for the absence of such an obviously practical and ingenious method of accurately securing a gun's fit are to be found in the almost total disappearance of the custom-built shotgun from the American scene. Repeating shotguns, almost by definition, do not lend themselves easily to custom styling if indeed they do so at all. The skyrocketing of custom-gun production, already discussed in the introduction as one of the principal reasons for the disappearance of the double gun from U.S. factories, would be just as prohibitive if applied to any other type of shotgun.

In a nation in which fine and traditionally-made double guns still exist and actually form a large part of the country's gun industry, it is to be expected that every effort will be made to secure as perfect a fit as possible to the customer's specifications. Where Rolls-Royce still produces cars to custom design and Bond Street Tailors still jealously guard their reputation for turning out the world's-best custom clothes, Purdey, Boss, Churchill, Lang, Greener, Powell, etc. certainly are still maintaining the traditional quality of the English double. Special adjustable guns are used or have in the past been used by these and all makers of top quality English shotguns.

So it is not unusual that Parker, in an effort to produce what was not only America's best shotgun but one best fitted to the customer's own needs and desires, should make use of the try gun. The photograph of this little-known item from the Parker factory comes from Lengerke and Antoine of Chicago and is here used by courtesy of that firm. Parker distributed this shooter's aid to the finest outlets for wonderful shotguns, such as Chicago's big V. L. and A. The try gun in the hands of a capable clerk was responsible for the best possible fit and was a tremendous assistance in not only ordering the desired gun but in satisfying a customer too.

These interesting details reveal several facts about the try gun. It was furnished to many dealers and distributors but the parts of one gun were never interchangeable with the parts of another. Care was necessary in the use of the gun as the adjustable parts were very finely and precisely balanced, making rough handling dangerous. The gun was, however, when properly used and adjusted quite safe for shooting and was often used for demonstration of the Parker's shooting qualities.

The movable measurement calculator made possible quick and minutely accurate determination of the prospective buyer's needs. The illustration of the try gun used by V. L. and A. shows a gun of V. grade and it seems probable that this special Parker was always made up in this grade. The V. grade reveals the fundamental design and quality of the Parker line and greater refinements would only have been a needless expense on a gun used purely for measurement and demonstration purposes. The Parker try gun adds an interesting chapter to the firm's history of striving for the utmost in a made-to-order shotgun, in addition to providing a particular gun which is certainly one of the rarest of Parkers and is not likely to ever find its way into the gun room of a collector.

The Parker Invincible

If the try gun and the very high grade Parkers are few in number and therefore rare, there is one Parker which is not only rare but is all but unique. It could, to be exact, be called "duique" with an unwarranted philological derivation of the Latin tongue, since only two of this model were made. The story behind this rarest of all Parkers is interesting, not only for the background it furnishes to the gun itself but for the information it reveals about the chronological progress of the company.

By 1928, the production figures at the famous Meriden plant had reached 190,000, not a staggering total by any means if compared to the production of the great gun factories like Winchester, Remington and Colt. But when it is remembered that these were factories whose lines were based on mass-production technique and that they included guns of many types while Parker had, from the beginning specialized in only one kind of gun and that of custom, hand-made quality, the sixty year total of guns turned out is nothing short of amazing. And so with this honorable record behind them and every prospect of an even brighter future, in 1928 the factory's staff of experts and technicians decided to celebrate a land mark which, so they easily calculated, was only two years in the future. There had been slight increases or decreases in recent production but the prosperity of the 1920's and the increase in popularity of

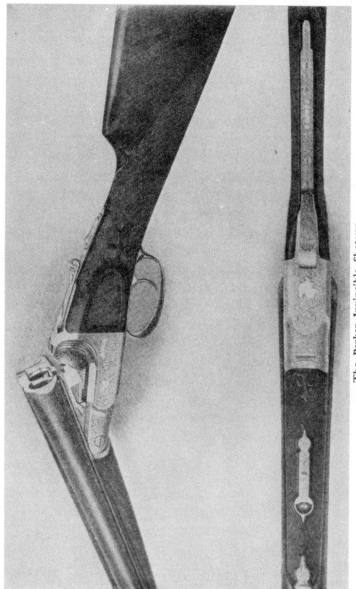

The Parker Invincible Shotgun.

shooting of every kind certainly made a yearly total of at least 5,000 possible. So as the fabulous twenties drew to a close and the factory approached the 200,000 mark Parker decided to mark the event by the production of what would be the ultimate in a shotgun. In short, Parker's craftsmen, technicians and artisans planned to outdo themselves. And they succeeded, although fate quickly decreed that the success would be short lived.

Since shortly after 1900 Parker had offered, as its finest gun, the A-1 Special. This was proudly claimed as a gun with no equal anywhere. But, for their 200,000th shotgun the factory offered not only an equal but a superior, The Invincible. This magnificent gun, pictured herein, is without doubt the finest, most beautiful, lavishly decorated and totally luxurious firearm ever produced in the Western Hemisphere. This is a large and rather extravagant claim but the facts support it. A glance at the illustration reveals the Invincible's incomparable artistry and sheer luxury. The price is final proof of the gun's place in the history of sporting arms. In 1930, when it came out, the Parker Invincible sold for $1,500, the highest figure ever charged for a shotgun produced in the U.S. When one remembers that this same gun, even were it possible to duplicate it today, would sell for at least three times that much, thus putting it ahead of even the most expensive English, Belgian, Italian and Austrian guns, the foregoing claim to its status is well authenticated.

To make only two comparisons, to the most expensive English and American guns of the same period, in 1930 the Purdey Shotgun was selling in New York for about 130 pounds, or about $650 at the most liberal rate of exchange, not including import duty. The L. C.

Smith Monogram Grade was selling for about $400, while Parker's most expensive gun in the regular line, the A-1 Special, sold for $750. Of course, the fact that the Purdey brought less in England than the top-grade Parker and L. C. Smith in the United States was simply the result of the fact that skilled labor was paid much less in England than in the United States.

But cost of production aside, the figure of $1,500 for a gun made in the United States, in 1930, is one which stands on its own record. By comparative value it has never been equalled before or since, nor has the product for which the sum was charged. I know of no shotgun made in either the United States or Europe at the time of the writing of this book (1959) which comes very close to equalling this figure even with the unprecedented wages paid skilled gun craftsmen here and abroad with the resulting unprecedented high prices charged for guns.

The price charged for the Invincible was not, however, made purposely high merely to give the gun a false commercial distinction. One thousand, five hundred dollars, representing work which today would demand at least four thousand dollars or more, was a perfectly reasonable figure, even in 1930, for the quality of work which Parker lavished on its *piece de resistance*. In this connection, it is well to mention at this point that a large profit is seldom if ever made on a very expensive gun. The majority of gun factories make their smallest profits on their most expensive models and their largest profit on the economy guns. Parker certainly found this to be true in the case of the Trojan and continued it until the rapidly changing economic conditions of the 1930's made further manufacture inadvisable.

It was, therefore, never the intention of the factory to make a "popular" gun of the Invincible. The technicians did, in fact, not anticipate that more than three or four a year would be sold. Events of a much broader nature, however, soon determined that not even that many would ever be made. Just as the Invincible was perfected and made ready for sale, at the height of the 1920's prosperity, the great stock market crash of October, 1929, brought the dream world that was then America to a close and with it the demand for such items as Parker's most beautiful and expensive gun. The Invincible was only offered publicly once—in the 1930 Parker catalog, dated January 1 of that last year of the delightful decade. The catalog had been planned and set up for release then and the stock-market crash had not prevented the release. But the aftermath of the crash soon brought an end to plans for further production of the Invincible. The Parker Company itself had only four and a half years more of independent life but did not, at the beginning of 1930, expect to go under completely. The very expensive guns, in any case, would not be in great demand and the most luxurious would have to be abandoned.

The Parker Invincible, numbered 200,000, was produced by the company after 62 continuous years of making shotguns. It was one of two models of this grade actually produced. Parker's 200,000th shotgun of pure luxury quality was a 12 gauge, with single trigger and straight stock. The checkering and decoration, of course, were lavish. The other specifications are unknown as it has been impossible to trace the gun itself. Even less is known about the second Invincible. Whether it followed the first in production and has the next serial number, the general design and specifications and the purchaser's name are all facts and details lost in the passage of the years. It is safe to say, however, that should either of the Invincibles ever come to the attention of any gun enthusiast or anyone with knowledge of the subject, he would have no difficulty identifying it. It is equally certain that no one who knows anything of shotguns would be likely to question the statement made by Parker in their comments on this beautiful and almost unique gun: "The discriminating gun lover will readily acknowledge the Parker Invincible to be the finest example of the gun maker's art ever produced by an American gun maker."

The Parker made for Tsar Nicholas of Russia

Mention has already been made, in the chapter on the Parker factory and employees, of the shotgun specially ordered for Tsar Nicholas II. Further details of this Parker, one of a large number specially ordered by many famous persons at home and abroad, may fittingly close this chapter on the Parker line.

Many of the books written about Tsar Nicholas and life at the Russian Court make allusion to the fact that the ill-fated Nicholas was fond of shooting and tennis, especially the former sport. At the royal summer palace, Tsarskoe Seloe, he would often take up his shotgun for random shots at crows and various small game. During the great Russian Winters, when he could manage to absent himself from his beloved wife and children, the Tsar hunted in Siberia, the Finnish lake district and other parts of the enormous empire of which he was the last ruler. For any European of the pre-World War

I era there was but one type of shotgun—a double barrel 12 gauge.

How Tsar Nicholas happened to order a Parker shotgun is not known. One very possible explanation is that the Tsar, who had many contacts and representatives in France, had been told about or even shown a Parker by one of the many Russians who had visited that country, from which more orders for Parkers were received than any other foreign nation. Or it is possible he was acquainted with the Parker by an American representative diplomatic or otherwise, in Saint Petersburg. Perhaps his desire was simply to have the finest shotgun each nation famous for gun making was capable of producing. Whatever the reason, he ordered his Parker through the Russian Consul in New York.

The gun, a magnificent A-1 Special 12 gauge, had a gold-trimmed stock of the finest and most beautifully finished imported walnut. The personal touch for the Tsar was the imperial Romanov eagle raised in gold bas-relief on the trigger plate. This Parker,. ordered by perhaps the most exalted head of state ever to select a shotgun from the Meriden factory, was destined never to reach its owner, on whom the cross of doom had fallen at just about the time the order was placed. Once the war clouds had begun to gather, Nicholas, still not fully aware of the events taking place around him, was soon involved in the inescapable net of horror which led him, and his whole household, to extinction in the basement of the old house in Ekaterinburg.

The gun made for Tsar Nicholas was disposed of in some other manner. To whom it was sold and who its present owner may be are facts which the author has been unable to determine. This royal Parker was last reported in the possession of a very wealthy resident of Long Island, New York, but inquiries have failed to turn it up there or elsewhere. Had history taken a different turn, this beautiful Parker gun would undoubtedly have become either a silent witness to the last days of the Russian empire and the last pleasures of its last Tsar or the companion of that tragic figure, who, had he and the family escaped the Bolshevick fiends, might well have spent many hours of retirement, roaming the fields of England, Canada, or even perhaps Vermont or Connecticut, carrying and shooting his Parker as he dreamed nostalgically of an empire and a throne that were no more.

NOTE: Since publication of the first edition of this book, several very interesting and unusual Parker Guns have come to the attention of the author. Among these is a beautiful 20 gauge A-1 Special, presented to Annie Oakley by Buffalo Bill Cody. This exquisite little gun is now in the possession of Dr. Robert Snavely of Hagerstown, Maryland. Another Parker, not merely unusual but in all probability unique, is a 24 gauge Trojan model. This extraordinary gun, owned by Robert Hoess of the Columbia Broadcasting System, Washington Bureau, was apparently the result of an experiment dealing with the manufacture of shells of this size. Never a widely used load anywhere, 24 gauge shells are now almost unknown except to collectors.

According to Mr. Hoess, his rarity was one of a group· of some dozen or so 24 gauge Trojans which Parker made up to the special order of the United States Cartridge Company. This firm, which made the claim that it would attempt the loading of any kind of ammunition at all possible, no doubt wanted a low cost but high grade shotgun for the ballistic trials of the projected new gauge. Whatever the results of the trials, no Parkers were ever made commercially in this bore and this special batch of guns, says Mr. Hoess, was then ordered to be destroyed. At least one, however, managed to survive. Here indeed is a collector's dream.

CHAPTER 10

Last Days of the Company and the Absorption by Remington

THE GREAT DEPRESSION which struck the United States in the final year of its most prosperous decade brought ruin and total obliteration to many businesses and manufacturing concerns of every type. For some the end was quick and final, for others a gradual process which took several or more years and in the final phase assumed the form of the loss of independent existence and absorption by a larger and financially more powerful concern. Parker Brothers ended by going the latter way. It is worthy of note here that, of all the many types of factories which the depression doomed, gun makers suffered less than almost any others which come to mind. No one gun maker was actually totally ruined by this era and all which were in business in 1929 were still in business, if only as subsidiaries, at the beginning of World War II. Many of the older gun makers had passed from the scene but their passing was due to circumstances certainly not connected with any form of depression, the most common reason having been competition of a kind which could not be sustained.

American double-gun makers were feeling the pressure of circumstances before Parker even thought of selling out. The old Baker Gun Company, which had turned out some excellent guns, had ceased operations around the early twenties. The A. H. Fox Company of Philadelphia had become a subsidiary of the Savage Arms Company several years before Parker was absorbed by Remington, for reasons not definitely connected with the depression. The demise of Fox is traceable by some to the over-buying of its production quota by a large retail concern. Ithaca was holding up as was L. C. Smith; and both would continue to do so until after the second World War, Ithaca to continue until the present as a maker of repeating shotguns.

For Parker, however, things were different. The factory's only type of gun was a specialty weapon of luxury or near luxury grade. Even the largest selling guns were of a price not approachable by many persons in an era when many homes across the nation found themselves with salt but no potatoes. If the Parker Gun had been made by a factory selling a much larger line of guns, or one including low-priced guns in its own line, the effect of the depression might have been different. But a depression economy could not sustain Parker quality and so the end of independent existence came before five more years had passed.

The immediate cause of the decision by Parker's Board of Directors to finally sell the gun business was the necessity of securing more money for other parts of the firm's extensive holdings. In this connection it should be remembered that in 1934, as in 1834, the Charles Parker Company did not confine itself to the manufacture of one item. The firm founded by the wise old Meriden industrialist had always followed the policy of manufacturing as large a variety of machinery and hardware as could be consistently sold with a sound

THE PARKER GUN

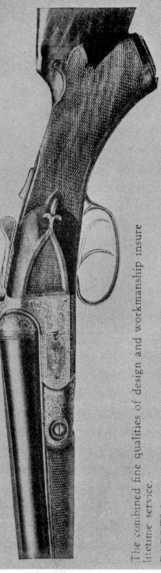

PARKER A H E
With Automatic Ejector

The combined fine qualities of design and workmanship insure lifetime service.

BARRELS —A steel manufactured for PARKER BROS. under our trade name—Acme.

STOCK —Carefully selected imported Walnut, beautifully checkered, gold shield, steel skeleton butt plate or rubber recoil pad Monte Carlo or cheek piece, if desired.

ENGRAVING—Richly engraved with scroll and game scenes.

SPECIFICATIONS

Straight or pistol grip. gauges, 10, 12, 16, 20, 28. Various weights, lengths, drops and measurements.

PRICES PAGE 15

The Parker A. H. E. as shown in the 1934 pocket catalog.

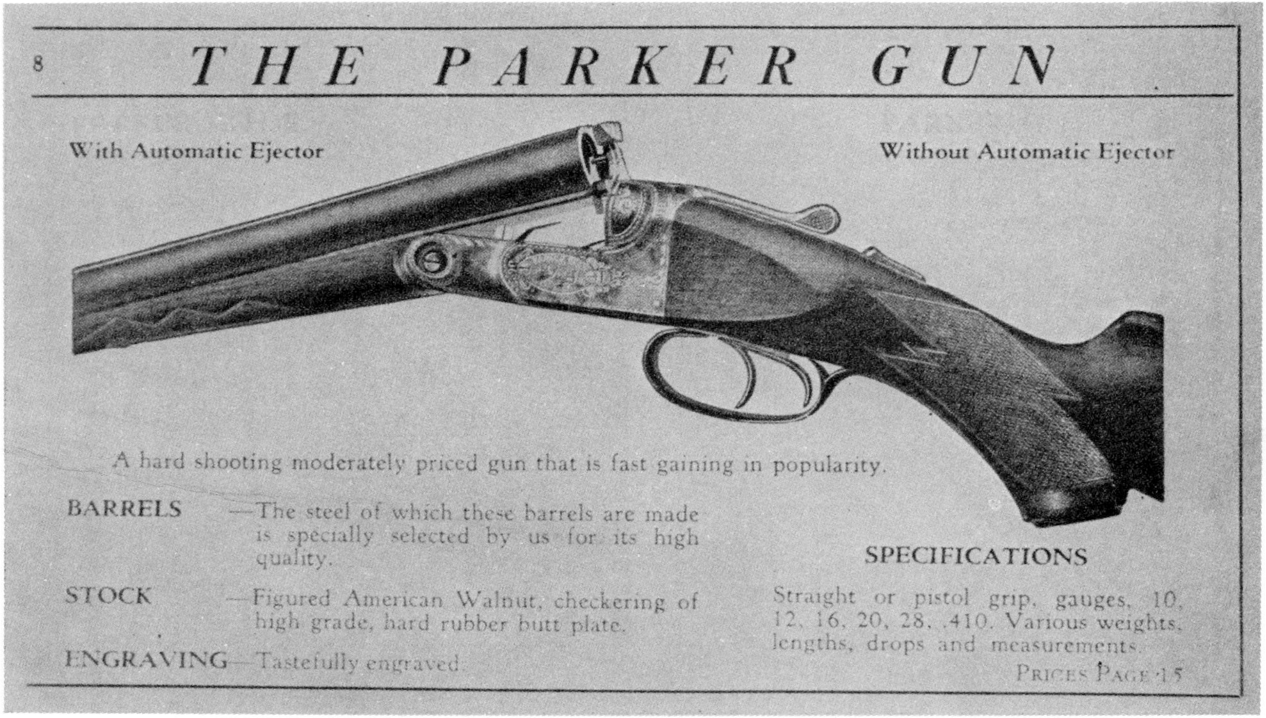
8

THE PARKER GUN

With Automatic Ejector

Without Automatic Ejector

A hard shooting moderately priced gun that is fast gaining in popularity.

BARRELS —The steel of which these barrels are made is specially selected by us for its high quality.

STOCK —Figured American Walnut, checkering of high grade, hard rubber butt plate.

ENGRAVING—Tastefully engraved.

SPECIFICATIONS

Straight or pistol grip, gauges, 10, 12, 16, 20, 28, .410. Various weights, lengths, drops and measurements.

PRICES PAGE 15

The Parker G. H. E. as illustrated in the 1934 pocket catalog.

THE PARKER GUN

PARKER V.H.E.
With Automatic Ejector

PARKER V.H.
Without Automatic Ejector

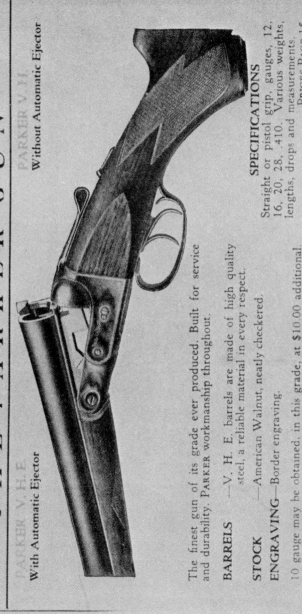

The finest gun of its grade ever produced. Built for service and durability. PARKER workmanship throughout.

BARRELS —V. H. E. barrels are made of high quality steel, a reliable material in every respect.

STOCK —American Walnut, neatly checkered.

ENGRAVING—Border engraving.

10 gauge may be obtained, in this grade, at $10.00 additional.

SPECIFICATIONS

Straight or pistol grip, gauges, 12, 16, 20, 28, .410. Various weights, lengths, drops and measurements.

PRICES PAGE 15

The Parker V. H. E. as shown in the 1934 pocket catalog.

THE PARKER GUN

Now furnished with New Improved Single Trigger at additional price of $26.00 Plus Tax.

Not Made With Automatic Ejector

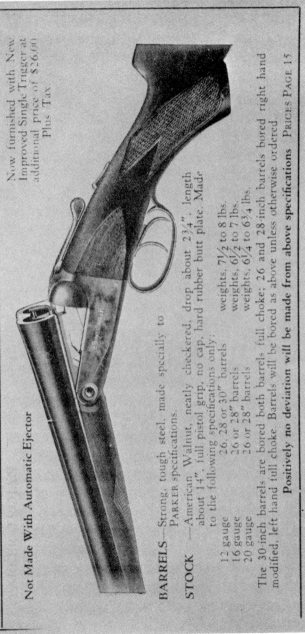

BARRELS—Strong, tough steel, made specially to Parker specifications.

STOCK—American Walnut, neatly checkered, drop about 2¾", length about 14", full pistol grip, no cap, hard rubber butt plate. Made to the following specifications only:

12 gauge	26, 28 or 30" barrels	weights, 7½ to 8 lbs.
16 gauge	26 or 28" barrels	weights, 6½ to 7 lbs.
20 gauge	26 or 28" barrels	weights, 6¼ to 6¾ lbs.

The 30-inch barrels are bored both barrels full choke; 26 and 28-inch barrels bored right hand modified, left hand full choke. Barrels will be bored as above unless otherwise ordered.

Positively no deviation will be made from above specifications Prices Page 15

The Parker Trojan as illustrated in the 1934 pocket catalog.

profit. In 1934, as always, the firm was quite cognizant of what the public was willing and/or able to buy, and the depression which started in 1929, after continuing for nearly five years, had proven that a gun of Parker quality and the necessary high price could not be made except at a loss which the business as a whole could not sustain. The only feasible course was to accept an offer by one of the larger gun firms and use the proceeds for the sustaining and improvement of the various parts of the Parker Company which could be reasonably maintained in the new type of economy.

Parker, at this moment, did not have to look at any great length for a prospective buyer. The firm had been eyed by larger gun makers for many years and had had several very attractive offers for the sale of its great shotgun. In the early 1920's, Winchester had become especially interested in buying the Parker Gun for its firearms holdings and had made a handsome offer. At the time, however, there was no necessity to sell as profits were good and Parker, like all American gun makers, was doing a good business entirely on its own. It was in consequence of Parker's refusal of the offer that Winchester developed its own Model 21 double gun, the gun which ironically enough, is, at the time of the writing of this book, the only high-quality double-barrel shotgun still made in the United States—and even it, as noted in the Introduction, is now a strictly luxury firearm available only on special advance order.

The depression had brought about in the firearms industry a price cutting war by certain gun makers whose production methods were such that they could reduce gun prices and still remain solvent. For Parker, however, no such course was possible because of the hand-made quality of its product and the fact that the Parker line only featured one type of gun.

It was, despite the pressure of the circumstances just mentioned, with reluctance that the Charles Parker Company finally, in 1934, decided to sell that part of the Company's business which had, during his liftetime, been the chief interest and favorite product of the founder of the gun division. Remington constituted a logical buyer, as it was large, had good investment capital, and at the time of the purchase did not feature even a low-priced double gun in its own line. Negotiations were concluded after the first of the year, just after Parker had released its last catalog as an independent company, the pocket catalog dated January 1, 1934.

So it was that on June 1, 1934, the manufacture and control of the Parker shotgun was assumed by the Remington Arms Company of Bridgeport, Connecticut, one of the nation's first makers of quality shotguns and rifles. The prices involved in the transaction covered both the actual Parker gun factory, its machinery, stock of parts and inventory of guns, and the complete rights to the name and symbols of Parker. The exact amount involved here is, of course, a company secret but it can be reliably assumed that some rather high figures were on the terms of sale. In particular, the price paid by Remington for the Parker name and the right to use it was certainly a phenomenally high one for the depression year of 1934. The fact that the name of Parker, as a symbol of all the gun had stood for throughout nearly seventy years, was worth such a high depression figure is as incontestable a proof as anyone could ask of the esteem in which the name Parker had come to be held by sportsmen and gun lovers the world over.

CHAPTER 11

The Remington Parkers

THE FINAL CHAPTER in the history of the Parker can be written almost entirely in terms of production figures and a change in geography. In the former case, we are at least fortunate in having available about the only exact figures on Parker production which research has brought to light. It is true that the records of Parker as an independent company, dealing with the gun practically from its creation, were maintained in Meriden and later preserved by Remington, but they constitute such an enormously complex area of research that an examination of any sort has proved a physical impossibility. When the change in ownership was made, however, some general statistics on the assets of Parker Guns were naturally assembled by Remington; and these survive, after a quarter century, either in the form of available records or in the memory of employees of both firms.

When Remington assumed control of Parker on June 1, 1934, no immediate changes were made in either the plant or its former methods and procedures. At the time, there were 104 completed guns in inventory ready for sale. In addition, there was a very large number of guns in various stages of completion plus a normal inventory of parts of all types. Subsequent to the date of sale, the Parker gun was manufactured for 3½ years at Meriden under exactly the same methods as the factory had used

209

as an independent firm. During this period of time, a total of 5,562 guns were produced in the Meriden factory.

At the end of 1937, Remington decided to close the Meriden plant entirely and transfer all Parker production to the main Remington factory at Ilion, New York. This was a move dictated by economic reasons, including greater efficiency in production. This does not mean, however, that the quality of Parker Guns was in any

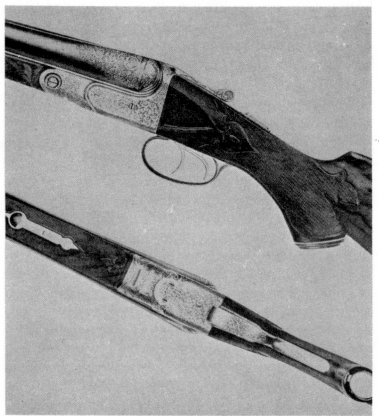

The A-1 Special as pictured in the 1937 Remington catalog entitled, The Parker Gun.

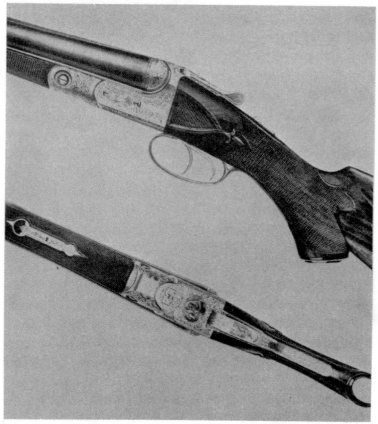

AHE Grade illustrated in 1937 Remington catalog.

way impaired or compromised. The question has long existed as to whether the Remington-made Parkers were of the same quality as those made at Meriden and as to what, if any, were the differences between the two. The answer, as indicated above, is most emphatically that there was absolutely no difference in the quality and that there are no differences in the Parkers made at Meriden and those made in Ilion, even in the markings and the serial numbers.

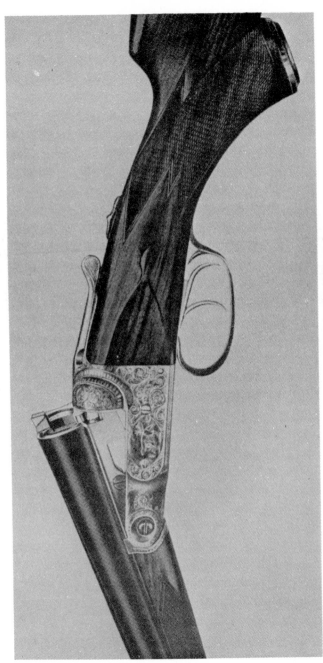

The D. H. E., as shown in the 1937 catalog.

The reason for this continuation of traditional quality was that, with few exceptions, all of the Parker employees with special skills and abilities transferred to
the Ilion plant and continued work on the gun as
usual. Approximately three-fourths of the entire factory
employment made the move to Ilion, and the absence
of those who, for one reason or another did not go, made
absolutely no difference in the gun's quality.

In 1938, full production of the Parker was resumed in
Ilion and maintained, on a greatly varying schedule,
until 1947. This latter date may well come as a surprise
to many who are under the impression that no Parker
guns were made after the mid or late 1930's. The fact is,
however, that Parkers were made in quantity through
the year 1943 and were either made up at odd times
or assembled from stock until 1947.

The aggregate Ilion production of Parkers was 1,723
guns. Of course, this figure does not seem at all impressive when it is remembered that it represents a total of
ten years' production, and that such a length of time,
during the factory's best days in Meriden would have
resulted in a total of at least 40,000 guns. The difference,
however, is easily explainable by two facts which surrounded the making of Parker guns at Ilion. The production schedule itself was a greatly reduced one, as it
had been ever since Remington took over. The figures
of Meriden production under Remington, 5,562 guns
produced in 3½ years, total barely one-third of Parker's
own top figures for a similar period. After the transfer,
it was only natural that production should drop off even
more, as Parker then constituted the strictly luxury item
in what was otherwise a large, modern mass-production
factory. In addition to production factors, the coming

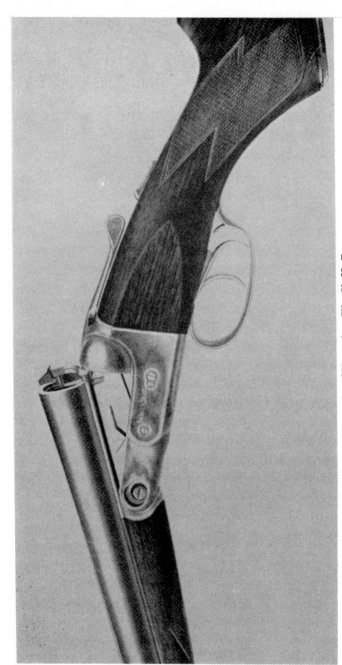

From the 1937 catalog, The V. H. E.

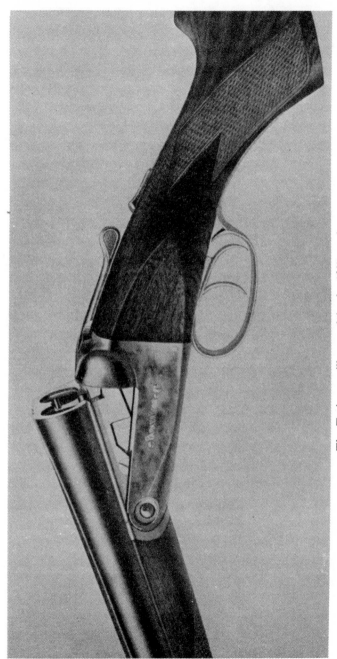

The Trojan, as illustrated in the 1937 catalog.

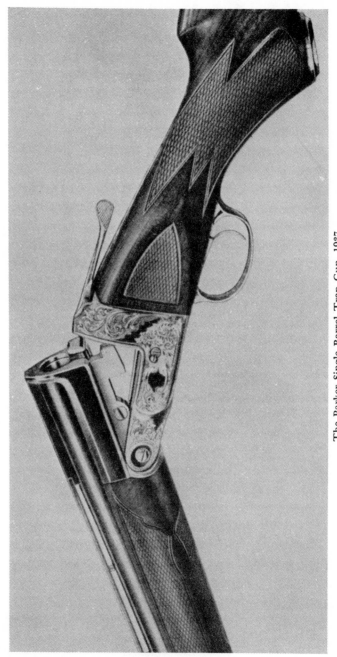

The Parker Single Barrel Trap Gun, 1937.

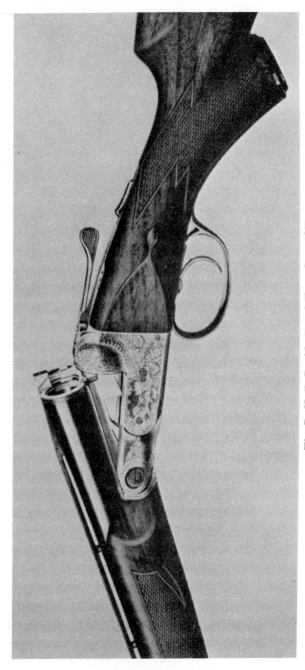

The D. H. E. Double Barrel Trap Gun, 1937.

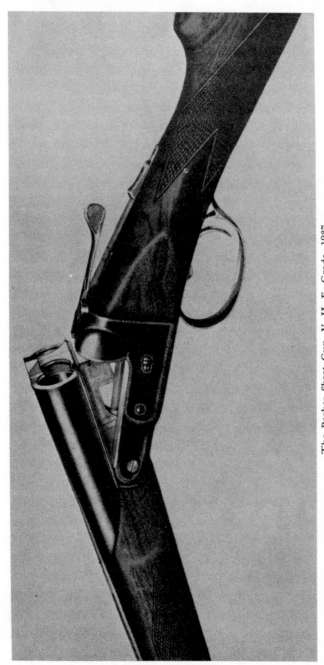

The Parker Skeet Gun, V. H. E. Grade, 1937.

of World War II late in 1941 naturally effected the production of guns after that time.

It is a curious fact, however, that the last production of Parkers, even on a very reduced scale, took place during the first two years of the war, at a time when the production of nearly all sporting arms had been completely halted. The explanation is probably to be found in the fact which dominated all Parker history—it was still a custom-made gun and did not require the use of much if any of the machinery which went into the factory's regular products, nearly all of which was required for defense work. In addition, the inventory of various parts kept in stock made possible the making of guns on an extremely small scale for about two years after the war started.

The Remington Parker was then made for a total of about ten years, including the $3\frac{1}{2}$ years Remington still maintained production at the Meriden plant, or from June 1, 1934 to about the same date in 1944. These dates do not take in the years to 1947, mentioned previously as the final years when Parkers were made, and this difference in time can be explained by the fact that, from 1944 to 1947, such Parker guns as were released by the factory were either assembled from parts previously in inventory, made to special order, or perhaps only paper transactions. Factory records do show, however, that the last year when any Parkers were made in number, however small, was 1943 and that the last Parker produced left the factory in 1947. So, depending on how the term "produced" is to be interpreted, the dates 1943 and 1947 may be taken as the terminal ones for the production of Parker shotguns. It is not known whether after this final Parker was completed any others

In the shop, 1937, barrel striking left to right: Frank Cashman, Sam Kencharek, Frank Wetzel, and John Geordel.

remained in inventory. If any did, they were certainly very few in number and did not last long.

It is now logical to sum up what is known of Parker figures. During the nearly eighty years of the great shotgun's life, a total of 242,385 were made. When the independent existence of the company came to an end in 1934, something over 230,000 had been produced; this plus the guns in various stages of completion, brought to 235,100 the exact number turned out by Parker Brothers as an independent firm. During the 3½ years, from June 1, 1934, to the end of 1937, 5,562 guns were made while the factory was still operating in Meriden. After all production was transferred to Ilion, 1,723 guns remained to be turned out.

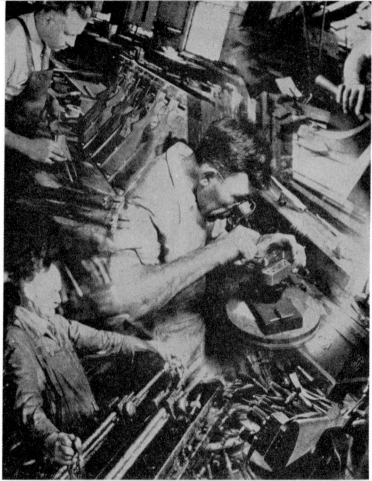

"Skilled Hands" as pictured in the 1937 Remington catalog, *The Parker Gun*.

The question has often arisen, in connection with the identification of Parkers, as to whether there is any difference in the identifying marks to be found on Parkers made in Meriden and those made in Ilion. The answer is apparently no. Serial numbers were strictly con-

Another illustration of "Skilled Hands" from the 1937 catalog.

tinuous from the guns made at Meriden to and throughout those made at Ilion. In addition, the proof marks used on the Ilion Parker guns were exactly the same as those used at Meriden. To complete the similarity, the gun-maker identification rolls whose marks are of course found on the matting rib between the barrels, are also the same for Parkers made at both factories. It is quite possible to find Parkers made in both places stamped either Parker "Brothers" or Parker "Bros." and the abbreviation of Connecticut as either "Conn." or "Ct."

The special machinery used to make Parkers was nearly all retained until the line was entirely discontinued. Machinery and equipment no longer needed for production is usually disposed of, and for this reason the Lefever Gun Works of Frankfort, New York, did acquire, at the time the Meriden plant was closed, at least two machines, one of which was for barrel matting and another a special machine used for an operation on a ventilated rib. In addition, a special machine used for one of the ejector operations was sold to a gun repair shop in the Ilion area. Otherwise, all special Parker machinery was kept by Remington until the gun was finally discontinued.

The exact circumstances under which the last Parker was made are, unfortunately, not known; and the records of its destination and exact specifications have long since been destroyed. It is not even known whether this last Parker was actually made in 1947 or whether it was an inventory gun which happened to remain on the shelf until this date. All that is known is the serial number: 242,385. Sometime in the year named, this final product of the greatest name in American sporting-gun making left the storeroom at the great Remington factory in Ilion and whoever now owns it may be proud that he has the honor of owning the last gun to bear the name Parker Brothers.

NOTE: Since publication of the first edition of this book, several Parker Guns have come to the attention of the author which are stamped with the name of Remington Arms Company and the address Ilion, N.Y. The descriptions of these guns have indicated, however, that such stamping was not on the identification found on the barrel matting rib but rather on the side of the barrel breech. Whether this reference to the name and address of Remington is to be found on all Remington-made Parkers, and if so, whether it is always in the same place, the author has not been able to determine.

CHAPTER 12

Conclusion

THE BUSINESS which Charles Parker started with one room and a blind horse in 1832, turned into one of the largest and most prosperous manufacturing concerns in New England, and guided into the perfecting and successful marketing of the finest shotgun ever produced in this hemisphere is its own monument to the genius, industrial wizardry and business acumen of the man who began as an apprentice button maker at 19 and lived into his 90's to be one of the wealthiest and most powerful of Connecticut's captains of industry.

The areas of hardware manufacture and marketing which have felt the influence of the name Parker are too numerous to make it worthwhile even to attempt to enumerate them. In the middle and later nineteenth century, in particular, there was scarcely a phase of the daily life of an average American for which the Parker firm did not make some kind of product. But with the possible exception of the coffee grinder, the one product of the Meriden plant by which the name of the founder has become almost a household word and certainly the one for which it will be longest known is the magnificent shotgun which the company's technicians turned out after the close of the Civil War.

Almost from the beginning the Parker held first place

among the half-dozen, fine-quality shotguns which the United States turned out during the half century or more when the double was king of the fields and ranges. The affectionate nick-name by which the Parker was known for so many years "the old reliable," was never more honorably earned by any mechanical product to which the name "reliable" has been applied. The original purpose which Charles Parker proclaimed, that of bestowing much effort to make the Parker what the sportsman needs, a good gun, was never deviated from in all the years the gun was made, nor was any deviation from the norm of quality ever considered when such a deviation was at all likely to compromise the gun's basic quality. Parker's slow and careful approach to any change or innovation, plus the most rigid inspection system of any gun factory in the United States, combined with the skill of the supreme Parker craftsmen and technicians to maintain the traditional Parker unchanged across the generations.

The many firsts which Parker perfected in the shotgun field testify well not only to the skill and devotion of the factory's employees but to their inventive genius as well. The 28 gauge gun, the beaver-tail fore-end, the ventilated rib, the unsurpassable bolting mechanism, the top grade luxury single barrel trap gun, all honors brought to the American gun industry by Parker will long remain among the most important additions to the perfection and advancement of the shotgun.

It is in the areas of actual usage, however, that the name Parker came to stand alone in the gun world. At the traps, in the skeet fields, and in every wood, field, meadow and duck blind where skill in gun making meant ease of handling, absolute dependability, and a well-placed shot, hunters and shooters said and still say, "If you've got a Parker, you've got the best."

It was unfortunately inevitable that a sudden change in the nation's economy which doomed many first class products and the mechanical changes brought about by a slow but steady change in sportsmen's preferences rendered the termination of Parker production unavoidable. And, although the shift in interest now is once again creating an interest in and demand for fine doubles, it is unlikely that it will ever be sufficient to cause the creation of a double of quality even approaching a Parker. Modern production costs are much too high to make such a gun practical even in a nation with a very high public buying power. But, more than the question of costs, the absence of the skill, craftsmanship and individual talent based on long, steady and individual pride render a gun of Parker quality almost inconceivable today and the likelihood of one ever being reissued decreases with every passing year as more and more of the older generation of gun makers join the passing parade.

The name Parker, and what it represented for so long, and still represents, remain to remind sportsmen and gun enthusiasts everywhere that here was the best in a sporting gun, and the Parkers still in circulation, destined by their quality to last for generations to come, will make those who are fortunate enough to own them proud of possessing American's finest shotgun.

CHAPTER 13

A Note on Buying and Collecting Parkers

THE COLLECTING of shotguns as a particular type of firearms has, to date, been the least popular of the many facets of the fascinating hobby of gun collecting. This is understandable in a sense, as the shotgun as a weapon does not offer either as wide a variety of mechanical variations or unusual and rare makes as do rifles or pistols. The best specimens are noted for their intrinsic quality and rarity of number, rather than for reasons which generally make guns attractive to the majority of collectors. And yet there are some few good collections of shotguns in the United States, and no doubt quite a few more in Europe. Certainly, the most widely-used type of sporting gun in the world has much to offer in the way of quality, rarity, and above all other weapons, classical beauty and aesthetic perfection of design.

Of all shotguns every manufactured in the Western Hemisphere, and among a considerable number in other parts of the world, none has so much to offer, not only to the shooter but to the collector and specialist as the Parker. It is, however, to the man looking for a top-quality shotgun to use that the Parker is most likely to appeal for quite a long time to come. Thus a word is here in order about the process of buying Parkers. Taking for granted that the prospective buyer knows just what type of double is best for the shooting he intends to do, the author of this book would remark, first, that anything outside of the commonest types of Parkers is going to be very difficult to find. It is common knowledge that very few stores have any choice of Parker guns available at a given time. In a large city it is uncommon to find more than two stores which have as many as three or four at once. Even the best of the smaller gun shops, in out of the way places, usually keep a waiting list for people desiring Parkers.

It is quite possible, however, to locate a good used Parker of the most often found grades at a fairly reasonable price. Specimens of the high and very-high grades do appear at times, but hard, extensive and often discouraging searching is usually necessary to find them. The price for such a Parker, on top of these considerations, is certain to be not only high but, except to a man to whom price is no object, almost prohibitive.

In my own many years of gun collecting I have only seen one Parker A-1 Special, and that was offered by Stoeger in New York at the beginning of the war, sometime in early 1942. The price then, of course, was only about seventy-five dollars more than the last retail price quoted by the factory, a little over a thousand dollars. What such a gun would sell for today is anyone's guess. They are hardly seen often enough to create the question of price, much less the actual opportunity for a sale. For anyone really interested, and with the necessary funds available, the best procedure is to check with the largest dealers in New York and Chicago and then to check the advertisements and/or to advertise for himself in the top gun magazines and trading papers.

But for the man who simply wants to own a Parker, and is satisfied with one of the less unusual varieties, a little searching, especially in the larger cities, will most likely turn up several good choices. The most frequently found Parkers are naturally those grades of which the most were made, the Trojan, the V. and the D. in that order. It is, at least in the author's experience, most uncommon to find any other grades in gun shops except in the largest cities. The most commonly found specifications will be 12 gauge, 28 or 30 inch barrels, and left modified right full choke. The would-be buyer of a Parker has one very great consolation in the purchase of whatever particular model happens to come his way: the chances are distinctly on the side of his getting a gun in at least good or probably very-good mechanical condition, one with good or usually much better bores and with at least fair finish and no rust. The reasons for this almost unique fact are simple: Parker guns were made to last a lifetime and, if given proper care, all of them will—hence, it is seldom if ever that a Parker is found with mechanical defects and loose breeches are unknown; most persons who were ever fortunate enough to own a Parker knew and cared enough about a good gun to give it proper care and maintenance.

Thus, while most Parkers are likely to have seen a good deal of service, the only real signs of even the hardest usage usually appear as surface wear. And this, fortunately, is easily corrected. At the time of the writing of this book, prices for the three grades of Parkers previously mentioned run somewhat as follows: the Trojan, from sixty dollars in good condition with worn finish to one hundred and twenty-five dollars in excellent condition with mint finish; the V. grade, from eighty-five to one hundred and fifty dollars, depending on condition and type of ejectors; the D. grade, from about two hundred and ten dollars to three hundred dollars depending on general finish, type of ejector, and specifications. Of course, it should be remembered that the particular dealer or source from which one obtains a gun will have a bearing on the price. If the man (or woman) desiring to own a Parker knows the line thoroughly he or she will usually be quite well aware of the values involved in any gun located.[1]

It should be mentioned that it is well to examine very carefully any Parker which chance brings your way. Do not, that is, reject one merely with a glance because it appears to be very worn or look as though it had seen some rough days. A dull or even badly worn surface may and quite often does hide a mechanically sound or very good interior. This, as previously noted, is a situation which is, in the majority of cases, easily remedied; however, a distinct word of caution is in order here. The re-bluing and refinishing of guns, particularly of high-quality double-barrel shotguns, is a process requiring skill that comes from long practice and experience. It is decidedly not a job for an amateur or any gunsmith not well versed in this kind of work. For that matter, in purchasing a used Parker or any other used gun, if there is any doubt whatever about the condition or reliability of the gun's mechanism have it checked by a reliable gunsmith. But in cases where a refinishing

---

[1] A check of prices, particularly those for 1940, the last pre-war year, will here prove helpful. Prices for this and other years are given in Appendix IV.

job is necessary be especially sure that the person to whom you entrust your gun is himself an expert in the art of bluing or sends such work to someone who is. Never take chances with this phase of gunsmithing.

To illustrate the point of what results may be obtained from the fortunate purchase of a Parker with a poor finish but in otherwise good shape, I may (with pardonable gun lover's pride) relate the story of the purchase of my own first Parker. In August of 1958, together with a friend, I visited the old Virginia City and Confederate Capitol, Richmond. While there, I made it a point to look up and visit as many gun shops as I could find. A shop dealing exclusively in gun repair and used guns, three sporting goods stores, one department store, another gunsmith, two pawnshops and a hardware store did not turn up a single Parker. Finally, on entering the last shop on my list, a pawnshop on Hull Street, I noticed at once a rack of double guns. The neat lines of two, in the middle of many other makes, at once proclaimed them to be Parkers. They turned out to both be Trojans and both priced at sixty-five dollars. I accepted the better-looking one after the dealer had reduced the price by five dollars, making the decision to buy after noting the good condition of the bores, the general good shape of the entire gun, and especially the excellent mechanical condition which included a crisp trigger pull and the proverbially tight breech.

After bringing the gun to Washington, I took it to a gunsmith who, I knew by reputation, to be one of the very best in the area and one with a large clientele. He pronounced the gun to be in very good mechanical condition and encouraged me to have it refinished completely. This task he divided between his own shop, where the stock and fore-end were completely refinished and the checkering re-cut, and a specialist in re-bluing. The latter expert lived in the mid-West and so the barrels had to be sent to him. When, three months later, I got the whole gun back, I could not believe it was the same piece I had bought in that Richmond shop. It is now one of the prides of my gun cabinet and shoots wonderfully well. The price of refinishing was fifty-five dollars, making the total cost of the gun one hundred and fifteen dollars. For this price I had thus obtained a gun which today it would take from three to five times that amount to make, if indeed such a mechanical creation were possible at all.

And herein lies the real value of a Parker to sportsmen and gun lovers of the present time. The quality of workmanship and individual craft put into each and every Parker could, today, not be reproduced in the United States (and hardly in many foreign countries) even if the price were not a factor likely to severely limit sales potential. The purchaser of a Parker is, for this reason, purchasing a product of an age which, for all practical purposes, has now passed away. He is buying the work of a factory which emphasized craftsmanship and quality to a greater extent than any other gun factory ever operated in this country, the product of a factory where, even in the case of the economy grade, every gun was a hand-made and hand-finished weapon. So, it should always be remembered, when anyone is considering the price of any Parker, that what the amount of money spent is paying for is, in reality, the great intangible of quality and skill, a quality and skill which are not only supreme but which will, in all probability, never be equaled in this country.

Collectors of shotguns, or anyone interested in acquiring extremely fine and rare guns, will naturally be interested in the particular Parkers most likely to be rarities, or of value and interest to the collector. In this connection, it may be said that the question can be approached from the standpoint of either grade or general specifications, in particular the gauge. If the general facts of Parker production are taken into consideration, it can be said that the following tables represent the order of rarity in the Parker line.

Grade	*Gauge*
The Invincible (of which only two were made)	10 gauge magnum
A-1 Specials	.410 gauge
AAH	.28 gauge
AH	

Try Guns:

Any high-grade Skeet or Trap guns, particularly the double-barrel trap model.

General Specifications

Any presentation model or gun created for a special purpose or occasion.

Any gun with barrels longer than 34 inches or shorter than 26 inches.

Any gun with stock or fore-end of markedly unusual design or dimensions.

Any gun which has been engraved or finished in an unusual or unconvential way, regardless of the purpose for which the finishing was done.

It is obvious that a Parker with Damascus steel barrels has a much lower value than any gun either of corresponding or different grade with modern steel barrels. Damascus steel Parkers, in fact, are not usually regarded as rare guns even if in excellent condition. But it goes without saying that this circumstance only applies to the lower grades which naturally are the ones most often encountered. Any A grade Parker, for instance, even though it had Damascus barrels, would be an extremely fine and rare item and one worth a good sum. In this regard, the older the gun the more valuable it will be, since the early high-grade models are especially desirable collector's pieces. In such a case, to the value of fine finish is added the extra distinction of age and early manufacture.

A word should be said also about the real antique Parkers, or those of the early under-lever lifter mechanism. These are so seldom seen as to be hardly worth looking for. Yet, there must have been at least some few thousands made. A very early Parker shotgun, in any condition, exhibiting the first type of mechanism used by the factory is a top-rank collector's rarity.

In regard to any Parker gun having Damascus barrels, a word of warning is here necessary. It would seem superfluous to say, after the same thing has been said so many times in so many other places, that modern shotgun shells must *never* be used in guns with Damascus or twist steel barrels. I think it pertinent to repeat and emphasize this fact in connection with Parker guns, however, for the following reason: because the very quality and strength of the Parker design and mechanism have become so widely known and admired, some persons are under the impression that it is safe to use modern shells in a Parker with Damascus barrels, especially if the gun is in good condition. In case anyone has received this impression elsewhere, or in the event that my own words of praise have seemed to imply that any Parker is safe to shoot, regardless of age or condition, let it be said most emphatically: no modern shotgun shell should *ever* be placed in a gun whose barrels are not of modern steel construction.

It is very easy to identify the old-fashioned barrels by noting the design of the finish and the identification stamp on the top rib. Any steel which is not of smooth texture, or which bears any reference to "Damascus," is of the older type and should not be used with any modern loads. If there is any doubt, consult a gunsmith.

A word should be said in conclusion about the identification and other marks to be found on Parkers. The name of the firm is always found on both the barrels and receiver. On the former part, it is stamped on the top rib and most often appears as:

PARKER BROS. MAKERS. MERIDEN, CONN.

As mentioned earlier, the word BROTHERS is often spelled out instead of abbreviated and the abbreviation for Connecticut, CT. In addition, the name and address are nearly always followed by the name of the particular kind of steel used in the barrel. For example, the Trojan is stamped TROJAN STEEL, the V. Grade VULCAN STEEL, the D. grade TITANIC STEEL, others ACME, SPECIAL, etc. Finally, the maker's identification on the barrel rib is preceded and followed by the tiny feathered arrow mark:

Both marks point inward. The maker's name on the receiver is, in all cases except the early guns, stamped on both the left and right sides as PARKER BROS. in old form letters. The only exception to this in the case of the more modern Parkers is the A-1 Special, where the name is stamped on the top front of the receiver.

The serial numbers on a Parker gun are usually found in four places: on the outside of the trigger guard extension in scroll form numerals, on the inside of the reverse side of the fore-end rib, on the left side of the locking lug, and the left side of the receiver water table. Sometimes a combination of two numerals is stamped on the rear of the locking lug, either the second and fourth, the third and sixth, etc. Directly beneath the serial number on the receiver water table is also stamped the grade letter of the gun, followed by an E when the model is equipped with automatic ejectors.

The patent dates of the Parker Guns are always found, on one or more places, on each model. The most prominent place is on the right side of the receiver water table where several dates are usually found, the most recent being in larger figures than the others. The older and perhaps the oldest of the dates is also commonly found on the left side of the barrel water table.

A very interesting form of marking found on Parker guns is the initial or initials of the barrel makers. Barrel making was one of the most highly skilled and demanding of the various crafts employed by the factory and the top men in this line often stamped their mark on what they turned out. WK or K stands for Walter King, and indicates that the barrels with these letters stamped on the water table were made by the son of the man who perfected the Parker gun after the Civil War. The letters JG stand for Jim Gary, another of the factory's best barrel makers. It is also quite common to find only the letter P stamped on the water table, simply indicating that the barrels were made and proved in accordance with Parker standards. Whatever the marks used, all Parker guns made since the turn of the century, and possibly for some years before, are stamped with some type of letter mark indicating the fact that the gun and its barrels passed the severest and most demanding inspection of any gun maker in the United States.

The location of the serial numbers in several places makes possible easy assurance that the parts of any Parker are all of a piece, and the interesting practice of the barrel makers stamping their initials on the barrel assembly will quite often reveal the fact that the barrels of an individual gun were made by a particular member of Parker's staff of expert craftsmen.

Parker Catalogs

A very important, and at times vital, aspect of collecting any type of guns is the study and use of catalogs. Indeed in recent years, so important has this part of firearms study in general become that dealers have arisen whose sole business is the acquiring and selling of old, rare and out-of-print gun catalogs from every corner of the globe. The collecting of gun catalogs has itself become an integral part of the process of both assembling and writing gun literature. This widely prevalent interest in old company publications relative to the countless makers of guns has gone far beyond the status of a hobby, fascinating though such a hobby is, and has now become an indispensable aid to the historical coverage of almost every type of firearms history.

The part played by Parker catalogs in this history of the Parker gun has been manifestly of paramount im-

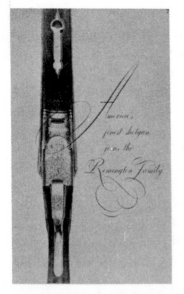

Reproductions of some of the Parker catalog covers in the author's collection.

portance. Without them no history of the gun could have been written. It seems therefore that something should be said regarding the status of Parker gun catalogs in relation to the collector of both Parker guns and Parker literature as well as the enthusiast whose hobby is the collecting of desirable gun catalogs in general.

And the first thing, unfortunately, which must be said in this connection is that, like the guns themselves, Parker literature of all types is extremely scarce and, when available at all, likely to be expensive. The author of this book has been, since the age of five, an avid collector of gun literature of every type and is the fortunate owner of a sizeable collection of gun catalogs, many of which are old and hard to find. But in all the years he has been collecting, the one and only Parker catalog which has ever come his way is the last one issued by the company while the gun was still being made and which was thus free on request at the time.

Out of dozens of lists of old gun catalogs and literature, some of them amazingly extensive, not a single Parker item of any nature has ever appeared. The amount of ordinary magazine advertising in even the most respected sporting journals was, as earlier mentioned, so small that a search for it in the world's largest library turned up almost nothing of value and precious little of any sort at all. About the only material ever available on the great gun was that issued by the factory from time to time in the form of standard catalogs with current price lists.

And the number of such catalogs issued, both in chronological series and total number of each issue, must have been always moderate and in some cases very small. The fact that so few of any year are available is an obvious indication of that. Catalogs were certainly not issued every year and there were apparently times when as long as five years passed without any new ones coming out. This was especially true of periods where there were no additions to the line and where economic stability kept prices unchanged for long periods. Here it is necessary to recall that the very fact that so few additions to the Parker line were made over the years would make yearly or frequent catalogs unnecessary. Any collector having any Parker catalogs or folders of any sort is very fortunate.

From the standpoint of the collector or Parker specialist, the most desirable of all Parker catalogs and literature is, by all standards, the 1937 catalog. This beautiful specimen of printing and advertising was, as earlier noted, the last Parker catalog or factory advertisement of any kind issued. It presents the line as offered by Remington the year when all manufacture had been moved to Ilion and the scope of the line had been extended to include the largest number of different hammerless guns ever offered under the Parker name at any one time. The line so displayed is quite representative of what the Parker line had been from about 1880 onwards and depicts the ascending grades of quality which had, from the beginning, characterized it. This catalog is, in addition, the only one displaying all Parker Trap and Skeet models.

Aside from the representative and comprehensive coverage of the guns in the line itself, the 1937 catalog is distinguished even more for the pictorial quality of its format. Printed on 11 by 8½ rag paper with gloss finish, and bound in mottled dull cream, the catalog is mounted in a spiral binding which appears in both wire and amber plastic form. Each model is pictured in a full length illustration, complemented on the opposite page by a circular-form sectional view showing a close-up of the central section including receiver, grip and forearm. The guns are reproduced in natural color against a neutral background. The sectional views reveal the richness and beauty of Parker engraving and checkering better than any other catalog or photographs of Parkers ever have. A valuable and unique feature of the 1937 catalog, herein reproduced, is the composite photograph adorning the center pages, which pictures some of Parker's finest artisans and craftsmen. This is the only such photograph ever used by the company in any of its advertising.

The credit for producing this outstanding gun catalog goes, of course, to the advertising section of the Remington Company Offices in Ilion. Prominent among the staff was Mr. Gail Evans, now the company's Director of Sales.

Other interesting Parker Catalogs are the 1899 issue, revealing the transition from the older mechanism to the modern line and listing the hammer and hammerless models, and the 1930 issue which is the only one to picture the Invincible. The former catalog, which is also interesting for its very detailed account of how Damascus barrels were made, is reproduced in full in John T. Amber's *The Rare Gun Catalogs,* publishing facts for which are mentioned earlier. The majority of Parker catalogs were about 8¾ by 7¾ in size and all that have come to my attention were printed on heavy, gloss paper. At least two, for 1917 and 1934, and possibly for other years, were pocket size.

The history of Parker, as of any gun, is well reflected in its catalogs and they all make highly desirable collector's items.

THE PARKER GUN

With Automatic Ejector

For the discriminating sportsman who appreciates the ownership of a gun of the highest quality of workmanship.

BARRELS —A steel manufactured for PARKER BROS. under our trade name—Peerless, of best quality and high tensile strength.

STOCK —Finest imported Circassian Walnut obtainable, beautifully checkered, solid gold name plate, triggers heavily gold plated, steel skeleton butt plate or rubber recoil pad

ENGRAVING—Individually designed, chosen for its simple richness, gold inlaying, engraved to customer's taste if desired.

SPECIFICATIONS

Straight or pistol grip. Monte Carlo or cheek piece if desired. Gauges 10, 12, 16, 20, 28. Various weights, lengths, drops and measurements.   PRICES PAGE 15

The Parker A-1 Special, the ultimate in Parker shotguns, listed in the last catalog issued as an independent firm, 1934.

Parker Family Tree

Charles Parker, founder of Parker Company. Son of Stephen Parker and Rebecca Ray. Controlling force of Parker Brothers Company. First Mayor of Meriden.
Born Cheshire, Conn., Jan. 2, 1809—Died Meriden, Conn., Jan. 31, 1902.

Wilbur Parker, proprietor of Magazine *American Sportsman.* After his death, wife (nee Lizzie C. Canfield) married again to Radcliffe E. Hicks, New England Sea Captain active in the China tea trade.
Born Meriden (date unknown)—Died in France when young (date unknown).

Wilbur F. Parker spent much of boyhood in France. During last years of the gun business was Vice President of the Parker Company in charge of Gun Operations.
Born Meriden, June 30, 1872—Died Meriden, Oct. 26, 1955.

Charles Stewart Parker, President of the Charles Parker Company, 1928-1933.
Born Meriden.

APPENDIX II

List of Known Parker Employees

H. L. CARPENTER—formerly general office manager for Parker Guns. Started with the Company in 1892. At time of the writing of the present book is 82 years old.

WILLIAM C. LIEDTKE—Master Engraver for nearly forty years. At time of writing, oldest known living Parker employee.

FRANK FAMA—Single trigger expert.

ROBERT RUNGE—an engraver, still employed by Remington.

A. D. KERR—A Remington employee who participated in transfer operations when gun business was sold to Remington. Was in residence for a time in Meriden.

MRS. MIKE HANSON—Started work with Parker in 1908 at the age of 16. One of the few women who stayed on the job as an actual gun craftsman. Did checkering of stocks and fore-ends.

THE STORMS, GEORGE, JEROME and FREDERICK—Master gunmakers, Frederick a particularly well-known barrel maker.

ROBERT REBSTOCK—foreman of the checkering staff, whose wife and sister-in-law were also checkers.

STANLEY PISARZ

HENRY NORTH

JOHN GEORDEL

RALPH FRANCIS

FRANK CASHMAN

FRANK WETZEL

FELIX BANNEK

FRANK SCHNICK

GOTTLIEB ANSCHEUTZ

ELBERT M. WEBB

SAMUEL KENCHAREK

JIM GARY

WALTER KING

LARRY DEL GREGO*

---

*Still employed by the Remington Arms Corporation, this master craftsman is assigned to work on Parker shotguns which are to be repaired. Mr. Del Grego can be addressed at 85 North Fifth Ave., Ilion, N.Y.

APPENDIX III

Table of Estimated Numbers of Each Grade of Parker Guns Produced

Because of the almost complete inaccessability of the production records kept by Parker as an independent firm, plus the even more unfortunate fact that the records kept by Remington after it purchased Parker have been almost entirely destroyed, even a closely approximate estimate of the number of each grade and type of Parker shotgun produced is, for all practical purposes, impossible. The task is rendered all the more difficult by the fact that the Parker office, while the firm was still part of the Charles Parker Company, kept no tables of the production figures which were broken down by grade or type of gun. In addition, the ledger entries for the guns, despite the fact that one was carefully recorded for each shotgun produced, are, even where accessible, extremely difficult to read because of the illegibility of the handwriting and other factors caused by age and storage. The destruction of the records of Parkers produced by Remington is especially unfortunate, since the exact specifications of the last Parker guns made would be of unusual interest.

Despite these difficult and adverse circumstances, however, a fairly good estimate may be at least attempted.

This is made possible by a calculation based on the known total of Parkers made in relation to the factory production policy of producing, each year, a certain percentage of each grade. It is obvious, of course, that this does not cover the very early figures when the Parker line had not been standardized to what it was by about the beginning of the 1890's. Only conjectures, based on the memory of older Parker employees, and approximate conclusions formed from various comparisons of figures, can give any hint as to the figures for early production of guns.

It should be emphasized, therefore, that the following figures are only estimates and may, in some cases, be wide of the mark.

EARLY MODELS
(Made between 1868-1888)	20,000
A-1 SPECIAL	320
A.A.H.	320
A.H.	5,600
B.H.	13,000
C.H.	5,000
D.H.	41,000
G.H.	28,000
P.H.	8,000
V.H.	58,000
TROJAN	50,000
LATER MODEL HAMMER GUNS	10,000

Note

From the above table, it would appear that more V. grade guns were made than of any other Parker, even the Trojan. Although this cannot be definitely substantiated, it is very likely the case. Facts tending to prove this are, that though the Trojan occupied the majority of each year's production from the time when it was introduced, it did not enter the line until 1915, whereas the V. grade had first been introduced about 1900 or just before. This means that V. guns, with both Damascus and modern steel barrels, were made for at least 15 years longer than the Trojan; and since, next to the Trojan, the V. was the best seller, it is apparent that for at least 15 years the V. grade was Parker's top-selling shotgun. Certainly, Parkers of the V. classification are just as often found as the Trojan and at times seem to outnumber it in availability.

I have not included figures for the E. and N. grade guns, since the fact that they are only listed in the 1899 catalog indicates that such a small number were made that even an attempt to estimate the exact figures hardly seems worthwhile.

Tables of Models and Prices as Listed in Various Parker Catalogs

1874 ADVERTISEMENTS

Gun listed only as available in "all the various styles."
Hammer models with lifter mechanism only.

Prices:	
$45.00	100.00
50.00	105.00
60.00	150.00
65.00	200.00
75.00	250.00
80.00	

1899

HAMMERLESS GUNS
(No Automatic Ejector)

A.A.H. Pigeon Gun	$400.00
A.H.	300.00
B.H.	200.00
C.H.	150.00
D.H.	100.00
E.H.	85.00
G.H.	80.00
N.H.	70.00
P.H.	65.00

HAMMER GUNS
(Top and Lifter Action, No Automatic Ejector)

A.A. Pigeon Gun	$400.00
A.	300.00
B.	200.00
C.	150.00
D.	100.00
E.	85.00
F. (Same as E. but straight grip)	80.00
G.	80.00
H. (Same as G. but straight grip)	75.00
I.	70.00
R.	60.00
S. (Same as R. but straight grip)	55.00
T.	55.00
U. (Same as T. but straight grip)	50.00

1912
HAMMERLESS GUNS

	With Auto. Ejc.	Without A.E.
A-1 Special	$393.75	$375.00
A.A.H. Pigeon	318.75	300.00
A.H.	243.75	225.00
B.H.	168.75	150.00
C.H.	131.25	112.50
D.H.	93.75	75.00
G.H.	78.75	60.00
P.H.	67.50	48.75
V.H.	56.25	37.50
D.H. 8 gauge	......	101.25
G.H. 8 gauge	......	90.00
P.H. 8 gauge	......	78.75

HAMMER GUNS

A.A. Pigeon	$300.00
A.	225.00
B.	150.00
C.	112.50
D.	75.00
G.	60.00
H.	63.75
R.	45.00
T.	41.25
D. 8 gauge	101.25
H. 8 gauge	90.00
R. 8 gauge	71.25

1915

HAMMERLESS GUNS

	With Auto. Ejc.	Without A.E.
A-1 Special	$400.00	. . . . .
A.A.H.	325.00	. . . . .
A.H.	250.00	. . . . .
B.H.	168.75	$150.00
C.H.	131.25	112.50
D.H.	93.75	75.00
G.H.	78.75	60.00
P.H.	67.50	48.75
V.H.	56.25	37.50
Trojan	. . . . .	27.50

HAMMER GUNS

A.A. Pigeon	$300.00
A.	225.00
B.	150.00
C.	112.50
D.	75.00
G.	60.00
H.	63.75
R.	45.00
T.	41.25
D. 8 gauge 34 to 36 inch barrel ..	101.25
H. 8 gauge 34 to 36 inch barrel ..	90.00

REVISED PRICES AS LISTED ON 1916 FLYER

D.H.	$101.25	$82.50
D.H. 8 gauge	......	110.00
G.H.	84.75	66.00
G.H. 8 gauge	......	100.00
P.H.	72.75	53.50
V.H.	60.25	41.50
Trojan	......	31.50

1917

SINGLE BARREL TRAP GUN

S.C.	$150.00
S.B.	225.00
S.A.	310.00
S.A.A.	450.00
S.A.1 Special	550.00

DOUBLE GUNS

A-1 Special	$600.00
A.A.H.E.	500.00
A.H.E.	340.00
B.H.E.	250.00
C.H.E.	182.00
D.H.E.	137.50
D.H.	117.50
G.H.E.	107.50
G.H.	87.50
P.H.E.	91.00
P.H.	71.00
V.H.E.	75.00
V.H.	55.00
Trojan	43.50

REVISED PRICES AS LISTED ON 1919 FLYER
SINGLE BARREL TRAP GUN

S.C.	$173.00
S.B.	260.00
S.A.	358.00
S.A.A.	520.00
S.A.1 Special	635.00

DOUBLE GUNS

A-1 Special	$725.00
A.A.H.E.	610.00
A.H.E.	410.00
B.H.E.	302.00
C.H.E.	220.00
D.H.E.	166.00
D.H.	142.00
G.H.E.	129.00
G.H.	106.00
P.H.E.	109.00
P.H.	86.00
V.H.E.	90.00
V.H.	69.00
Trojan	54.75

1930

INVINCIBLE—No price listed in catalog, but two
made sold for $1,500.00 each.

SINGLE BARREL TRAP GUN

S.C.	$160.00
S.B.	210.00
S.A.	350.00
S.A.A.	525.00
S.A.1 Special	625.00

DOUBLE GUNS

		With Single Trigger
A-1 Special	$750.00	$796.00
A.A.H.E.	625.00	662.00
A.H.E.	425.00	457.00
B.H.E.	300.00	332.00
C.H.E.	215.00	245.00
D.H.E.	160.00	190.00
D.H.	135.00	165.00
G.H.E.	115.00	143.00
G.H.	95.00	123.00
V.H.E.	87.00	115.00
V.H.	68.00	96.00
Trojan	55.00	......

1934

SINGLE BARREL TRAP GUN

S.C.	$176.00
S.B.	231.00
S.A.	385.00
S.A.A.	577.50
S.A.1 Special	687.50

DOUBLE GUNS

		With Single Trigger
A.1 Special	$825.00	$875.00
A.A.H.E.	687.50	728.20
A.H.E.	467.50	498.30
B.H.E.	330.00	360.80
C.H.E.	236.50	267.30
D.H.E.	176.00	206.80
D.H.	148.50	179.30
G.H.E.	126.50	155.10
G.H.	104.50	133.10
V.H.E.	98.70	124.30
V.H.	74.80	103.40
Trojan	60.50	89.10

1934 REMINGTON FOLDER

SINGLE BARREL TRAP GUN $176.00—$687.50
DOUBLE GUNS

		With Single Trigger
A-1 Special	$825.00	$875.00
A.H.E.	467.50	498.30
B.H.E.	330.00	360.80
C.H.E.	236.50	267.30
D.H.E.	176.00	206.80
G.H.E.	126.50	155.10
V.H.E.	95.70	124.30
Trojan	60.50	89.10
V.H.E. Skeet Special ..	......	139.15

1937

REMINGTON-PARKER CATALOG
(Last Parker Catalog Issued)
SINGLE BARREL TRAP GUN

S.C.	$191.00
S.B.	256.00
S.A.	415.00
S.A.A.	612.50
S.A.1 Special	725.50

DOUBLE GUNS

		With Single Trigger
A-1 Special	$890.00	$942.00
A.A.H.E.	735.00	776.50
A.H.E.	515.00	547.00
B.H.E.	375.00	407.00
C.H.E.	275.00	307.00
D.H.E.	198.00	230.00
D.H.	169.00	201.00
G.H.E.	134.00	162.60
G.H.	112.00	140.60
V.H.E.	100.40	128.00
V.H.	79.50	108.10
Trojan	72.50	101.10
V.H.E. Skeet Special	......	168.45
V.H.E. Double Barrel Trap Gun	......	200.45

FEBRUARY 16, 1940
PARKER-REMINGTON PRICE LIST
(Last Publication of Parker Guns, Equipment and Prices)

SINGLE BARREL TRAP GUN

S.C.	$225.00
S.B.	290.00
S.A.	449.00
S.A.A.	646.50
S.A.1 Special	761.50

DOUBLE GUNS

		With Single Trigger
A-1 Special	$890.00	$942.00
A.A.H.E.	750.00	791.50
A.H.E.	530.00	562.00
B.H.E.	390.00	422.00
C.H.E.	290.00	322.00
D.H.E.	195.00	227.00
G.H.E.	159.00	187.60
V.H.E.	139.00	167.60

PARKER SKEET GUNS

V.H.E.	$182.45
G.H.E.	202.45
D.H.E.	246.00
C.H.E.	347.00
B.H.E.	451.00
A.H.E.	593.00
A.A.H.E.	829.50
A.1 Special	988.00

PARKER DOUBLE BARREL TRAP GUNS

V.H.E.	$215.45
G.H.E.	235.45
D.H.E.	276.00
C.H.E.	382.00
B.H.E.	486.00
A.H.E.	628.00
A.A.H.E.	875.50
A-1 Special	1,034.00

As noted in the chapter on the Parker line, all guns offered in the 1940 Price List were available with such extras as the beavertail fore-end, raised ventilated rib, and a set of interchangeable barrels which included a regular fore-end.

Prices for such extras were graduated according to the grade of the gun for which they were ordered, ranging, in the case of the beavertail fore-end, from $14.85 for the V.H.E. to $46.00 for the A-1 Special; in the case of the raised ventilated rib from $27.50 for the V.H.E. to $46.00 for the A-1 Special; and in the case of a set of extra barrels from $72.00 for the V.H.E. to $390.00 for the A-1 Special. On the two lowest grades, the G.H.E. and the D.H.E., certain other extras such as a soft rubber recoil pad, a skeleton steel butt plate, oil finish for the stock, and any deviations from the standard dimensions of the stock, brought an extra charge; while from the D.H.E. on up these could be had to the customer's specifications at no extra charge.

Bibliography

The number of books containing even a significant mention of Parker guns is small. Only the following are worth mentioning and even they have only a very small amount of information.

Askins, Charles: *The American Shotgun* (New York: Outing Publishing Company, 1910).

————: *Modern Shotguns and Loads* (Marshallton, Delaware: Small Arms Technical Publishing Company, 1929).

Keith, Elmer: *Shotguns* (Harrisburg, Penna.: Stackpole Company, 1950).

Colonel Arcadi Gluckman's excellent book *United States Muskets, Rifles and Carbines* (Stackpole Company, 1959) has good detailed notes on the rifles Parker produced for the government during the Civil War.